Scale Your Way to

Music Assessment

G-7068

SCALE YOUR WAY TO
MUSIC
ASSESSMENT

THE ULTIMATE GUIDE TO CREATING A
QUALITY MUSIC PROGRAM

PAUL KIMPTON
AND DELWYN L. HARNISCH

GIA Publications, Inc.
Chicago

G-7068

GIA Publications, Inc.
7404 South Mason Avenue
Chicago, IL 60638
www.giamusic.com

Printed in the United States of America.

ISBN: 978–1–57999–636–9

CONTENTS

Foreword

by Judy Arter

I have yet to meet a teacher that doesn't want students to take control of their own learning, to become life-long learners, or to care more about the learning than the grade. The issue is what to do in the classroom to accomplish these things. It doesn't work just to say, "Okay, students, you will now take control of your own learning." We as teachers need to have strategies to teach students how to be independent learners, and we need to incorporate certain types of assessment activities into the classroom that automatically shift the focus from the grade to the learning. That's what *Scale Your Way to Music Assessment* is about: fostering student independence, improved achievement, and motivation to learn through the powerful strategies of assessment for learning.

Think back to your own experiences in school. Think of a time when assessment was a distinctly negative experience for you. What caused the experience to be negative? What was its effect on you as a learner?

Educators who answer this question typically report that negative experiences with assessment tended to be caused by such things as not knowing what a test would cover, trick questions, results reported back in an embarrassing or demeaning way, incomprehensible or no feedback, feedback delivered too late to do any good, test questions seemingly unrelated to what the teacher said was important, poor quality or confusing test questions, and comments intended to justify a grade rather than to aid improvement. Effects tended to be things like embarrassment, anger, giving up, never talking in class again, and never taking another class in the subject. The teachers of these respondents probably didn't mean to have these effects; such effects are inadvertent. Nevertheless, educators can't afford to have students who make unproductive decisions about learning, whatever the cause.

Now think of a time when assessment was a distinctly positive experience for you. What caused the experience to be positive? What was its effect on you as a learner?

Educators usually report that the following features of assessment lead to positive assessment experiences:

- What was to be tested was clear
- Clear criteria for success
- Feedback usable to improve performance
- Personalized feedback
- Practice similar to assessment even if not graded
- Step-by-step learning aligned with assessment
- Understandable questions
- A chance to improve before the final grade

Educators report that the impact of these features of assessment are increased motivation, increased learning, increased appreciation of the subject, and good rapport with the teacher.

Thinking through positive and negative experiences with assessment highlights the relationship between assessment and student motivation. Quality assessment is not just about getting accurate information about students, although accuracy is certainly essential. As Rick Stiggins, a colleague, says, quality assessment is also about engineering assessments and associated procedures to cultivate productive responses on the part of students regardless of their current level of achievement. A productive response looks like the following:

- I understand the results
- I understand what I need to do next
- I'm okay
- I choose to keep trying

An unproductive response is the opposite:

- I don't understand the results
- I don't understand what I need to do next
- I'm probably too stupid, anyway
- I give up

No one will argue with these ideas. The question becomes what specifically one should do day-to-day in the classroom that will have these positive effects. Research (e.g., that summarized by Black & Wiliam, 1998, and Hattie & Temperley, 2007) over the past twenty-five years indicates that assessment for learning strategies has dramatic effects on student learning and motivation because they enable students to take control of learning by promoting understanding of where they are at a point in time and what to do next. Further, the largest gains are for the lowest achievers.

Assessment for learning is the process of using assessment materials, procedures, and results to boost student achievement during the learning process. This can be compared to assessment of learning, the purpose of which is to summarize and make a judgment about the adequacy of each student's achievement after learning is supposed to have occurred. Assessment of learning includes grading, interim assessments, and course or year-end tests. Assessment for learning includes actions on the part of both teachers and students. Teachers might give assessments at the beginning of the school year or course to determine what students need to work on, give assessments during the course to track student progress and plan educational experiences, and use assessment to provide descriptive feedback to students on what they are already doing well and what they should work on next. These actions require a clear statement of what students are to know and be able to do by the end of instruction, day-to-day use of assessments that provide accurate information about what students are doing well and what needs to be worked on next, mechanisms for helping teachers to use information to promote learning, and sound feedback to students (Hattie & Timperley, 2007).

Student assessment for learning actions include self- and peer-assessment, analyzing results of assessment, making decisions about what to work on next, and tracking their own progress. In order for students to be able to do these things, they must also have a clear understanding of the learning to be done and be accurate assessors of that learning. The idea with student involvement is that the person doing the work does the learning.

This manual provides practical guidance in all these areas for music education. Several sections are devoted to assistance with making learning goals for students clear, relating content standards and how students might use and play music as adults, and tracking across courses and grade levels. There are also sections on how to accurately assess various learning goals, including listening, extended written response, and performance assessment.

But the best parts are those having to do with assessment for learning: specific guidance on teacher use of information to improve student learning and student involvement. *Scale Your Way to Music Assessment* describes in detail how to teach students to use the NFHS music adjudication form criteria to help them become not only accurate and consistent assessors of musical performance, but how to meaningfully self- and peer-assess and set goals for practicing and improving the performance of a group. This includes a year-long schedule of assessment for learning events by teachers and students, and forms for practical data analysis and recording.

The result is a manual that attends to both accuracy and effective use of assessment to promote rather just measure student achievement in music.

An important question (dealt with in the introduction) is this: Is the goal of music education to create independent musicians or just good performances? If the goal is to create only good performances, educators should take students out of the loop as much as possible, because, presumably, they know more about how to create a good performance than students. But, if educators want to create good musicians, students need to be in the driver's seat. Assessment for learning teaches them how.

Judy Arter is author and consultant
for Educational Testing Service

PREFACE

Yesterday is gone. Tomorrow has not yet come. We have only today.
Let us begin.

Mother Teresa (1910–1997)
Missionary and winner of the Nobel Peace Prize

As I sat on my screened porch, thinking about how to begin *Scale Your Way to Music Assessment*, I reflected on all the people who influenced my early musical life. I thought about my father, Dale Kimpton, who was inspired by many great teachers as a young trumpet player and as a music education major at Northwestern University. I thought about the musicianship rating system that he created and that I grew up with in Quincy, Illinois. Every time I look back at the teachers and experiences that made a difference in my life, a common thread is evident: they all challenged me to learn and apply information on a higher level. But more importantly, they taught me to assess myself and my performances and to listen to others' assessments of my efforts in order to truly reach my potential. This background is what drives me today to gain new knowledge and to use it not only to create a better me, but also to help others reach their musical potential.

Assessment is here to stay! Educators can use this tool to become better teachers—true music educators—who will change their practices and methods as well as the practices and methods of their students. The goal of *Scale Your Way* is to show the positive results of assessment, which will quickly dispel the negative reactions to assessment.

As you move through each chapter, you will hear two distinct voices. The first voice is written from Paul Kimpton's viewpoint as he applies the basic concepts of assessment to a music program. The second voice is Delwyn Harnisch's, and takes a wider view of assessment and what research and other assessment experts have to say about assessment in education. Having these two perspectives allows you to see the journey the authors went through in creating music assessments for the arts.

ACKNOWLEDGMENTS

A book is the sum of the author's support group, just as a concert is the sum of the performers. My support group began with my parents, providing me the opportunity to learn music and absorb their philosophy of education, be it at the dinner table or anywhere we gathered. Although they have since passed away, their passion for music education and life live through the words I have written.

Administrators past and present also played a part in my career in education. I must thank Joseph Dalpiaz, a great educator and my former principal, for hiring me at Hinsdale South High School. That one moment was a turning point, as it allowed me to join the great tradition of excellence at Hinsdale South. Additionally, I have had the pleasure of working with numerous district administrators: three superintendents, John Thorson, Roger Miller, and Nicholas Wald, who provided outside experts to expand our minds and ideas in education; three assistant superintendents, William Trescott, Jim Polzin, and Kevin Probst helped lay the groundwork for our district initiatives and kept us on track; in addition to Dalpiaz, Steve Walton and Claudia Geocaris were Hinsdale South principals who supported my assessment work, but more importantly, supported my daily work as a teacher and Department Chair at Hinsdale South.

I also must thank Jerry Bellon for coming to our district and challenging us to create goals and objectives that would drive us to be better teachers and administrators.

Implementing an assessment program required an open-minded staff who learned to use assessment to improve instruction and student performance, and these educators should be commended for taking an idea and helping make it a reality.

I thank the one with whom I have shared thirty-six years, my wife, Ann Kaczkowski Kimpton. She has been my editor for thirty-six years both in writing and in life. She edited, challenged, encouraged, and above all supported me in this project, as in everything we have done as a couple and as a family.

Teresa Edwards was not only the editor for the first edition, but is also a close friend who supported me in developing *Scale Your Way*'s first edition. Gregg Sewell at GIA has been the editor for the second edition and has helped to make *Scale Your Way* a clearly written and useful tool for music educators.

Alec Harris of GIA publications saw the potential of *Scale Your Way* for music education, and is thanked for putting his company's time, money, and energy into producing a quality product.

Finally, my co-author, Delwyn Harnisch, has worked through the editorial process by sharing updates, analyses, and chapter edits, while enhancing my understanding of assessment. I want to thank him for helping get this project to you, the reader. Through this endeavor, I wish to share my father's dream—that everyone experiences

"A richer, fuller life through music."

—*Paul Kimpton*

I would like to acknowledge the professional learning community that was formed under the leadership of Roger Miller with his colleagues at the District 86 Hinsdale Township High School District. Opportunities for professional development were supported that focused on building high-quality local assessment and connecting them to teacher leadership. Paul Kimpton took it to heart and shared it with his students and developed a passion for excellence that was contagious and has spread among colleagues and many music educators in the United States.

The vision that Paul and I share in *Scale Your Way* is drawn from the collective wisdom of many. I was blessed to have been given the opportunity to work with a team of outstanding teachers from whom I learned many lessons. The players on this team include Jim Polzin, John Brunsting, David Anderson, Suzanne Strohschein, Jeff Waggoner, Claudia Geocaris, Susan Camasta, Kathy Gabric, Kevin Pobst, John Naisbitt, Tim Shimp, and other colleagues from both high schools at Hinsdale. The team members each brought their perspectives to the assessment round table for review and building ownership of next steps for student involvement and improved student achievement.

Others have assisted by giving comments on earlier chapters. Primary among these are Mitzi Hoback, Jan Hoegh, Ron Shope, Fred Ritter, and my students, Kristi Bundy and Darin Kelberlau. The text has been improved markedly by their insightful comments.

—*Delwyn L. Harnisch*

INTRODUCTION: LET US BEGIN

How would you answer the following questions?

Do your students have musical content knowledge and the ability to apply that knowledge independently? If your students are unable to read music independently or participate on a very high level in other musical groups, are you helping to develop true musicians?

Performance is the driving force behind most music programs. This one word propels us to ignore the other important force—the performer, or what we will refer to as *Independent Musicians Creating Quality Performances* (IMCQP). Music teachers will do anything and everything to make a performance a success. They will sing parts to students instead of having them learn to read notes and rhythms. Directors will play the same songs for months until the students can play or sing the music without any understanding of how to apply what they have learned. Departments will have no lesson plans or curriculum for the day, week, month, and year except to play the music in rehearsal.

How should music educators define *successful performance*? We believe assessment to improve student understanding and application is why we as educators should assess.

If we make assessment separate and unconnected to our students and curriculum because we are forced to do so by our school or state, then we should not assess. Of the utmost importance, however, is our commitment to developing Independent Musicians Creating Quality Performances (IMCQP) who are well educated in performance, theory, and music appreciation. These young people are the future supporters and consumers of a very precious art form; they are our legacy for the future. Assessment must be one of the tools in a process that gets us to the goal of creating IMCQP.

Assessment for musicians does not need to lag behind the other disciplines in a school district. Musicians have been assessing performance skills, performances, and written musical knowledge for years. The problem is that we as a community of music educators have not taken the lead in sharing what we currently are doing and putting it into a clear and measurable system. Current researchers in classroom assessment have found ways to encourage high- and mid-range achievers to grow even faster, while at the same time preventing low achievers from giving up. Research conducted by Crooks, Black & Wiliam, Harnisch, Shope, Hoback, and Fryda & Kelberlau in the United States and around the globe reveal that the way to maximize learning is not to maximize anxiety, but to maximize students' beliefs that they can and will learn if they keep trying. According to *Learned Optimism: How to Change Your Mind and Your Life*, (Seligman), we must redefine the relationship between assessment and student motivation to one in which we use assessment, not to build the confidence of some and destroy the confidence of others, but instead to build every student's belief that he or she can learn, to build each student's sense of academic optimism.

Scale Your Way will guide you through the steps in creating both performance and written assessments for your music programs. *In Classroom Assessment for Student Learning: Doing It Right—Using It Well* (Richard J. Stiggins, Judith A. Arter, Jan Chappuis, and Stephen Chappuis), the authors suggest using assessments that will:

Encourage, not discourage
Build confidence, not anxiety
Bring hope, not hopelessness
Offer success, not frustration
Trigger smiles, not tears

In addition to helping music educators, *Scale Your Way* is written to help your administration understand and develop a cohesive assessment program to improve student musicians' performance and understanding.

Answer this question before going on to the next chapter: How does an assessment plan help music educators develop more effective instruction that leads to increased student understanding of music and better student music performances?

The eight notes of the F scale will be our musical guide to remembering and creating music assessments. Let's begin this exciting project by looking at each of the steps.

FIGURE 1.

"Give a man a fish and feed him for a day: teach him to fish and feed him for a lifetime." I think this proverb should say, "Give a student a musical answer and you have gotten him through one day's rehearsal; teach a student how to read, assess, and perform music on his own, and you create a musician for life."

HOW TO USE THIS BOOK

Del and I, along with the staff at GIA publications, have made every effort to provide music educators with a wealth of information and materials for creating, understanding, and implementing a written, listening, and performance assessment program. These materials will help you formulate your own ideas as you read the book.

First, peruse the appendixes, including the sample written and listening tests and performance expectations. In Chapter 4, several suggestions for assessment software, music theory software, workbooks, and test-making software are discussed. We have included the websites for these companies, and invite you to go to these sites and download the samples there and become familiar with some of the many options available to you. If you already have software, by all means begin using it, as you may use any software you want to complete your assessment program. Also included with the book is a disc from *Music Performance Assessment Experts* (MPAE). The MPAE disk provides templates and sample tests that may be edited to fit your needs. These tests were made with Sibelius software, but PDF files are also included if you do not own Sibelius. The graphs and charts were developed using JMP. If you go to the JMP website (http://www.jmp.com/), you can download a thirty-day working copy of the data analysis software that was used to make the charts and graphs included here. The MPAE disk has sample test data in Microsoft Excel format for you to use with the JMP program.

If you have Sibelius software installed on your computer, open the four sample written and listening tests to get an idea of the music content (Chapter 2) and test format. To help you create your own tests, several blank templates are included on the accompanying disc. If you do not have Sibelius software, PDF copies of the tests are included on the MPAE disc. The only difference between these and the Sibelius files is that you will not be able to edit the tests without retyping them.

Audio files are included on the MPAE disc as well. Turn to the sample listening test in Appendix E and open the corresponding audio file on the disc so that you can see how the audio file and hardcopy go together. A listening test script is included on the sample disc. The script text was formatted in Microsoft Word and is included so that you can easily edit it.

Next, return to chapter 9 and briefly look at the graphs and charts of longitudinal data that we gathered over years of performance evaluation. Chapters 8 and 9 further explain how the data was gathered and used to improve instruction. Don't worry if you have questions; once you read *Scale Your Way*, these chapters will help you better understand assessment terminology, data analysis, and the qualities of valid and reliable tests.

As you go through the sample disc, you will also see templates for goals and objectives, lists of musical skills, and sample test data to help you create your own data tables and graphs. Please feel free to copy the forms, worksheets, and the test free of charge.

Support groups are important for music educators who often feel isolated. The message board at our website (www.mpae.net) allows you to post a question which will be answered by the authors in addition to giving other educators a chance to respond to your questions. Many schools are doing great things with assessment, and you will find that you are not alone in this pursuit. Our website also has a list of dates and times when you may call and talk to Paul Kimpton on the phone for further help. As you work through each chapter, please share with us your questions and experiences so that we may help you on your journey of creating a comprehensive music assessment program.

Scale Your Way is designed to be used in many different ways, and targets three distinct communities of music educators: music education professors, K–16 music educators, and pre-service music educators. For the next several pages we will discuss in greater detail how each group can benefit from *Scale Your Way*.

MUSIC EDUCATION PROFESSORS

Assessment is an effective tool at the higher education level to motivate and instruct students in solid assessment practices. If colleges and universities use an established assessment system with their students, major benefits can be realized. The music education students will witness firsthand how instructors adjust lessons and teaching strategies based on student performance. They will also learn how to implement a total assessment program from beginning to end.

As explained in the Preface, *Scale Your Way* provides an actual example of a school that has taken assessment theory and applied it in practice. Software is included with this book so that students can develop data analysis skills. Giving students the opportunity to dialogue about improvement of instruction before entering the world of teaching may allay some initial fears of implementing an assessment program. Students will learn how to look at data objectively, not personally. Other areas of use for *Scale Your Way* in a music education methods class may include how to:

- Write music curricula
- Write goals and objectives
- Understand data terms
- Use data to improve instruction
- Interpret student data
- Interpret teacher data
- Align curricula
- Use assessment software
- Create written, listening, and performance assessments
- Understand assessment practices

K–16 MUSIC EDUCATORS

The second community involves current K–16 music educators, the front-line troops in the battle to save music education. These educators face ever-growing pressure to use assessment in the classroom and defend the importance of music in a child's life. *Scale Your Way* details the ammunition: the curriculum, objectives, goals, performances and test data that illustrate student and teacher growth in a music program. These powerful results give teachers the necessary data to justify music as a curricular essential. Teachers need to see how a working assessment program is developed and how assessment results are used daily to improve instruction. By following the steps in *Scale Your Way* to develop an assessment program, teachers are able to adapt these ideas to their particular schools and communities without having to start from scratch. We have spent twenty years developing this program; we want teachers to take our ideas to new heights.

Additionally, creating a department assessment program will help unify the music staff, which often sees itself as vocal versus instrumental. This divisiveness is a major problem in music education. *Scale Your Way* encourages dialogue and collaboration among staff members in order to create an educational climate that focuses on student musicians. Students, parents, and administrators will see the music department as having a well-defined educational atmosphere that makes student achievement its number one priority. The administration will also see that the arts can document student musical growth and track it longitudinally. Other uses of *Scale Your Way* in a K–16 setting may include how to:

- Write music curricula
- Write goals and objectives
- Understand data terms
- Use data to improve instruction
- Interpret student data
- Interpret teacher data
- Align curricula
- Use assessment software
- Create written, listening, and performance assessments
- Understand assessment practices

PRE-SERVICE MUSIC EDUCATORS

The last community, the music educators of the future, is the most important group of all. Young educators who enter the field often have limited exposure to music programs in other schools. This narrow experience often results in a first-year teacher trying to duplicate his or her high school or college experiences. *Scale Your Way* provides novice teachers with another model to consider when designing a total music assessment program.

SCALE YOUR WAY TO MUSIC ASSESSMENT

Examples of worksheets, software, and assessment data are here for prospective teachers, along with examples of good assessment practices and the steps in their creation.

Young educators have a very tough job indeed, often having groups perform just weeks after the opening of school. Furthermore, they must teach students how to improve individual musical skills. In order to survive short-term performances, they may forget the long-term goals of teaching musical skills. *Scale Your Way* helps new teachers create a balance between performing and developing musical skills. Other uses for *Scale Your Way* for pre-service or novice teachers may include how to:

- Write music curricula
- Write goals and objectives
- Understand data terms
- Use data to improve instruction
- Interpret student data
- Interpret teacher data
- Align curricula
- Use assessment software
- Create written, listening, and performance assessments
- Understand assessment practices

CHAPTER 1
FORGET THE BAGGAGE

Have you ever talked to a person or department member who had so many pre-conceived ideas or negative opinions that it was impossible to move ahead in a discussion? We often find ourselves carrying around years of experiences or baggage which have a negative influence on our everyday lives and relationships. These experiences also cause us to not look at ideas objectively. So let's get rid of the baggage to begin our musical assessment journey. Let us share a few common examples of baggage before you make your own list.

FIGURE 2.

Everyone has some type of baggage that will surface as you begin to work as a department. Use the guidelines below as your "Robert's Rules" for assessment discussions.

- Don't let your personal past experiences get in the way of department discussions.
- Keep the focus on what all musicians should be able to do.
- Brainstorm: Time is not a problem if you see the bigger picture and are organized.
- Don't talk about what you think, but rather about what student musicians need.
- Don't get into a vocal versus instrumental discussion. (Musicians are Musicians.)

Here are some ways to get this project started while keeping the focus on:

- Student Musical Understanding (SMU)
- Student Performance Skills (SPS)
- Independent Musicians Creating Quality Performances (IMCQP)

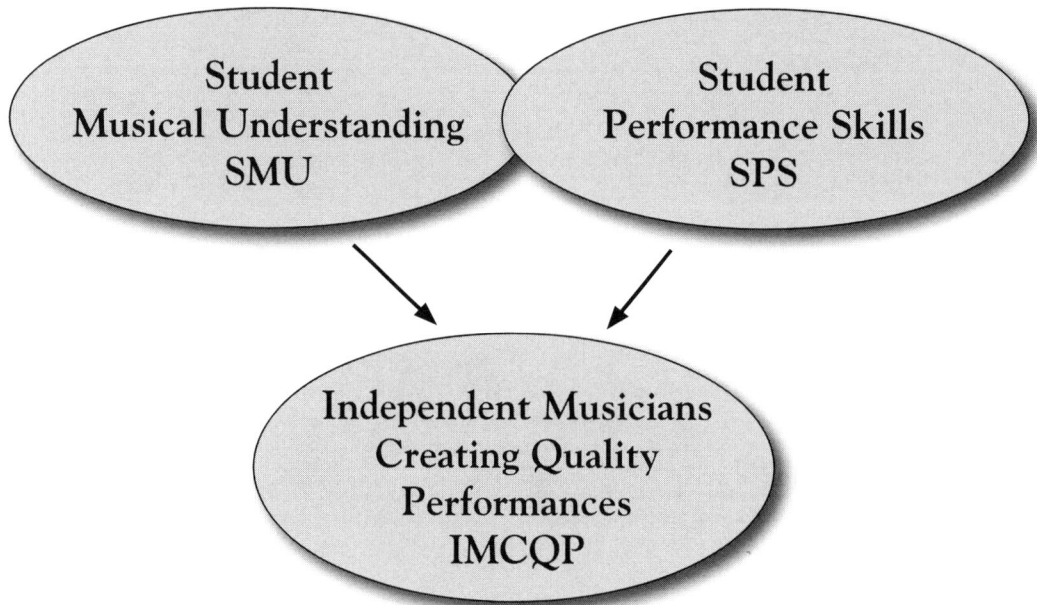

FIGURE 3.

TAKING NEGATIVE IDEAS AND CREATING POSITIVE EXPERIENCES

One of Paul's best educational experiences was when he was working on his counseling/guidance certification. During counseling sessions, he would ask students to write about their feelings and to look at problems in a variety of ways. The physical and mental process of putting feelings or thoughts on paper increases awareness and insight into negative feelings. Taking a negative feeling and restating it in a positive way allows individuals to deal with negative issues and move ahead, not letting the issue inhibit their lives. Students who were able to see options to negative influences in their lives made the most progress. Paul applied this strategy to his own work and music staff discussions on developing a music assessment program. He found that there were negative issues about assessment that needed to be resolved in order to move ahead as individuals and as a department.

In the next several pages you will write your feelings and thoughts about assessment so that any negative feelings your music staff has can be discussed and resolved to avoid inhibiting your efforts to develop an assessment program.

Whatever you are, be a good one.
Abraham Lincoln (1809–1865)
16th President of the United States

PART 1

Photocopy the next few pages. Gather all teachers in your department. On the lines below, ask each teacher to make an individual list of negative feelings or reasons for not wanting to have a music assessment program.

1. _____

2. _____

3. _____

4. _____

5. _____

6. _____

7. _____

8. _____

9. _____

10. _____

PART 2

Have everyone read their lists aloud and explain why they wrote each reason. Remember to just listen with an open ear and not interrupt. Once all have shared their lists, copy all the comments into one list in the space below and on the template on the accompanying disc.

1. _____

2. _____

3. _____

4. _____

5. _____

6. _____

7. _____

8. _____

9. _____

10. _____

11. _____

12. _____

PART 3

Now write the reasons for creating performance and written assessments. Here is an example to get you started:

"Creating written and performance assessments will allow us to have a department curriculum that will focus our teachers, students, parents, and administration on the goal of creating independent musicians."

1. _____

2. _____

3. _____

4. _____

5. _____

6. _____

7. _____

8. _____

9. _____

10. _____

PART 4

The next time you get together, have everyone read the completed list of personal baggage. Agree that these can never be used again as a reason for not moving forward in this exciting project.

Have your department's personal list of baggage at every meeting.

SUMMARY

You and your department have finished Step 1: Forget the Baggage in *Scale Your Way to Music Assessment* and should feel ready to get to work as a unified group of music educators. You have looked deep into your feelings about assessment and your philosophy as music teachers. You have openly shared your feelings with colleagues, and in doing so, you have opened your mind and heart to seeing music education and assessment in a positive light. You are finally ready as individuals and as a department to help students reach their potential as performers and musically educated young adults.

We hope you will visit our website (www.mpae.net) and share with us and others how your musical journey is going. Let us congratulate you and give you feedback as you develop an assessment plan.

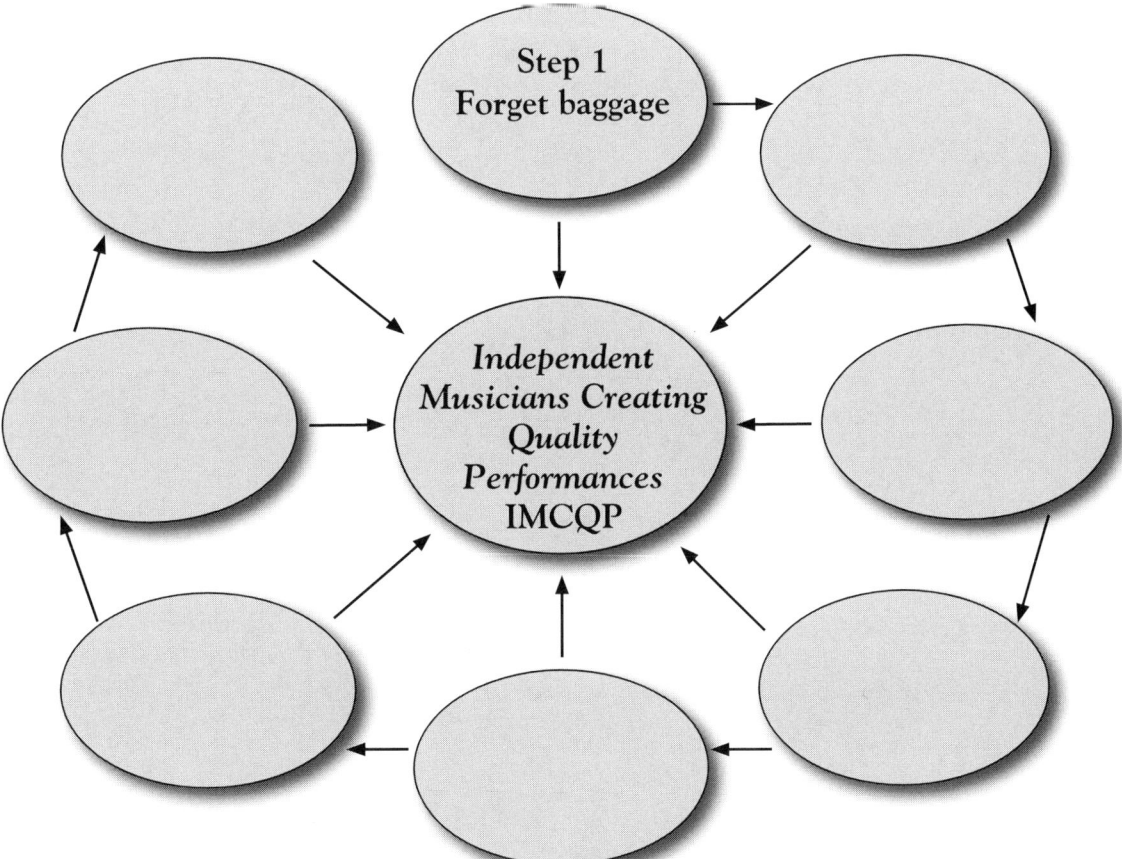

CHAPTER 2
GENERATE A LIST OF MUSICAL SKILLS

In 1988 we began working on what the State of Illinois called local assessment. Local assessment was our state's way of saying, "We can't come up with a state test for the arts, so you decide what your students should be able to do and then create ways of measuring those skills." In these discussions, we always came back to the same question:

What do we want students to learn
and how do we know they learned it?

These discussions caused us to realize that our department had not established a clear set of musical skills for each year students were in the program nor a method for measuring where each student was in mastering those skills. In addition, the administration, students, teachers, and parents were not aware of what skills were needed to become independent musicians during the time they were in the program.

In the next several pages you will be asked to answer questions about how music skills relate to skills in other disciplines. These questions will help you understand that each school discipline, sport, or almost any other activity has a certain skill set needed to perform that task on a high level. Once you have answered these questions, you will begin developing a list of skills and discussing with all members of your department what all musicians should know and be able to demonstrate vocally and instrumentally. If your school or faculty is small, then consider visiting and talking to other music educators. Create a network of music teachers with whom you can share your ideas and opinions. If you are unable to connect to other educators, then go to our website (www.mpae.net) and share your questions and ideas on our message board. Let the other educators that participate there help you with your journey.

If you question whether having a set standard for musical and performance skills is necessary, try the following exercise. Read the five questions, write a short reaction to each, and discuss them as a department or with a colleague.

1. How can a student go through four years of choir and not be able to read music and prepare music outside of class?

   _____

   _____

   _____

2. Can you imagine going through four years of math and not being able to do math unless a teacher guides you through math problems? Does this sound like some music classes you have seen?

   _____

   _____

   _____

3. In some instrumental and vocal rehearsals, we put the strong musician in the middle of the section so other students can follow instead of teaching everyone to read. Remember in high school, you have them for four years.

   _____

   _____

   _____

4. Can you imagine an English class in which the best writer sits in the middle of a group of poor writers? The weaker writers look at what he writes and copy it. How is this similar to weak singers following a better singer instead of learning how to read music as an individual?

   _____

   _____

   _____

5. How do you explain a percussionist moving from the fifth through the twelveth grade and only being able to play a snare, not being able to read treble clef (mallets), bass clef (tympani), or not being able to count rhythmic patterns?

_____

_____

_____

These questions will stimulate your department to look at students differently. We leave you with one last thought:

Is the goal to create a good performance or a good performer?
We think the goal should be both.

Now that you have read and discussed these statements, answer the following questions.

1. Do your students understand and can they articulate the skills needed to become independent musicians?

2. Can you prove and show on paper and through individual performances what skills your students have mastered?

3. Do you have a written curriculum that you could hand a parent, administrator, or new teacher in your department that shows what each of your classes will be doing for the year and how skills will be measured?

4. If any of your faculty left, would you be able to show incoming teachers a list of the skills of returning students? Would you be able to hand them a curriculum to show them what should be taught in each class and a timeline for when the skills should be taught?

These statements and questions should help your department have some valuable discussions. When you are ready, the next step is to tackle the most important aspect of the assessment journey: your department's list of musical skills.

PART 1

Discuss with all members of your department what all musicians should know and be able to demonstrate vocally and instrumentally. At this point we really need to see that all musicians are created equal. Yes, even drummers and vocalists.

Answer this question:

What are the Student Musical Understanding (SMU) and Student Performance Skills (SPS) needed for students to understand and perform music on their own? To become Independent Musicians Creating Quality Performances (IMCQP)?

Student Musical Understanding (SMU)	consists of listening (aural), music theory, music terms/vocabulary, and genres
Student Performance Skills (SPS)	skills demonstrated through playing or singing

SPS consist of:
- *Tone quality*   resonance, control, clarity, focus, consistency, warmth
- *Intonation*   accuracy to printed pitches
- *Rhythm*   accuracy of notes and rest values, duration, pulse, steadiness, correctness of meters
- *Technique (facility and/or accuracy)*
  artistry, attacks, releases, control of ranges, musical and/ or mechanical skills
- *Interpretation/musicianship*
  style, phrasing, tempo, dynamics, emotional involvement
- *Diction*   vocal
- *Bowing*   strings
- *Articulation*   winds

- *Other performance factors*
    choice of literature, appropriate appearance, poise, posture,
    general conduct, mannerisms, facial expression (vocal), memory
- *Scales, intervals, triads*

Figure 5 presents a partial list of skills to consider. On the disc that accompanies *Scale Your Way* there is a Microsoft Excel spreadsheet with a more complete list of skills to help you get started.

Remember to meet as a department to discuss musical skills and vocabulary for all musicians, not just skills needed only by vocal students, or only instrumentalists. Often we have no control over what students learn before they come to our class, so make your list assuming they don't have the skills you think they should have. Keep baggage out of the discussion and focus on what all musicians need to know and be able to do.

Your list can be made as a group or each person can use the template on the acccompanying disc to create an individual list. This assignment can then be turned in and pasted into a complete list.

The template in Figure 4 has six sections. Each section is discussed in detail as you are asked to complete that portion of the template.

Skill or Term	Volume No.	Year Taught	Year Tested	Objective No.	Assessment Type					
					W	L	IP	S	F	DF
					W	L	IP	S	F	DF
					W	L	IP	S	F	DF
					W	L	IP	S	F	DF
					W	L	IP	S	F	DF
					W	L	IP	S	F	DF
					W	L	IP	S	F	DF
					W	L	IP	S	F	DF
					W	L	IP	S	F	DF
					W	L	IP	S	F	DF
					W	L	IP	S	F	DF
					W	L	IP	S	F	DF
					W	L	IP	S	F	DF
					W	L	IP	S	F	DF
					W	L	IP	S	F	DF
					W	L	IP	S	F	DF
					W	L	IP	S	F	DF
					W	L	IP	S	F	DF
					W	L	IP	S	F	DF

W • Written   L • Listening   IP • Individual Performance   S • Summative (Sum)

F • Formative   DF • Department Final

FIGURE 4.

MUSICAL SKILLS AND VOCABULARY TEMPLATE

Written (W), listening (L), Individual Performance (IP), Summative (S), and Department-ment Final (DF) assessments are performed to determine the overall effectiveness of an educational program.

PART 2

Have each person in your department read his list and give a reason for including each skill. Remember to listen only and don't interrupt; you can always add and delete later. Once each person has shared her list, use the on-disc template to make a combined list of all skills and/or terms. Sort the list alphabetically and delete any duplicates.

Figure 5 presents a partial list. Note that the second column (Volume No.) gives the volume number of the theory program we use. This makes it easy for students and teachers to find the section of the theory program material in which the skill or term is treated. No entry in this column indicates the term/skill is not in the program or will not be tested. Chapter 6 is devoted to details of the theory program we use.

Skill or Term	Volume No.	Year Taught	Year Tested	Objective No.	Assessment Type					
1st and 2nd endings	1				W	L	IP	S	F	DF
1st inversion	3				W	L	IP	S	F	DF
2nd inversion	3				W	L	IP	S	F	DF
3rd inversion	3				W	L	IP	S	F	DF
8va					W	L	IP	S	F	DF
AB (binary) form	3				W	L	IP	S	F	DF
AB motive					W	L	IP	S	F	DF
AB ternary					W	L	IP	S	F	DF
ABA (ternary) form	3				W	L	IP	S	F	DF
ABA binary					W	L	IP	S	F	DF
ABA rondo					W	L	IP	S	F	DF
Accelerando	1				W	L	IP	S	F	DF
Accent	1				W	L	IP	S	F	DF
Accidental	1				W	L	IP	S	F	DF
Accompany	3				W	L	IP	S	F	DF
Adagio	1				W	L	IP	S	F	DF
Aeolian mode	3				W	L	IP	S	F	DF
Alla breve	2				W	L	IP	S	F	DF
Allegro	1				W	L	IP	S	F	DF
Allegro moderato					W	L	IP	S	F	DF
Andante	1				W	L	IP	S	F	DF
D. C. al coda					W	L	IP	S	F	DF
Perform all ascending intervals (major, minor, diminished, augmented)					W	L	IP	S	F	DF
Perform all ascending major and perfect intervals					W	L	IP	S	F	DF
Perform all major and minor descending intervals					W	L	IP	S	F	DF
Perform all minor scales					W	L	IP	S	F	DF

W • Written   L • Listening   IP • Individual Performance   S • Summative (Sum)
F • Formative   DF • Department Final

Figure 5.
Musical Skills and Vocabulary (Partial List)

SUMMARY

Look back at the first two steps you have taken. You have gotten rid of your negative feelings about assessment listed in Chapter 1 (Forget the Baggage) and have channeled your energy into working toward the goal of creating Independent Musicians Creating Quality Performances (IMCQP). Next, in Chapter 2 you listed the Student Performance Skills (SPS) needed to make an independent musician. This gives you an opportunity to reflect on what you had to do to become an independent musician yourself, which will help you to better understand what all students should understand and be able to do in their journey to become independent musicians.

You should have completed a list of skills and written them down. These two completed steps show how much you have learned and how far you have come as you *Scale Your Way to Music Assessment*. They also provide the foundation for the next six steps.

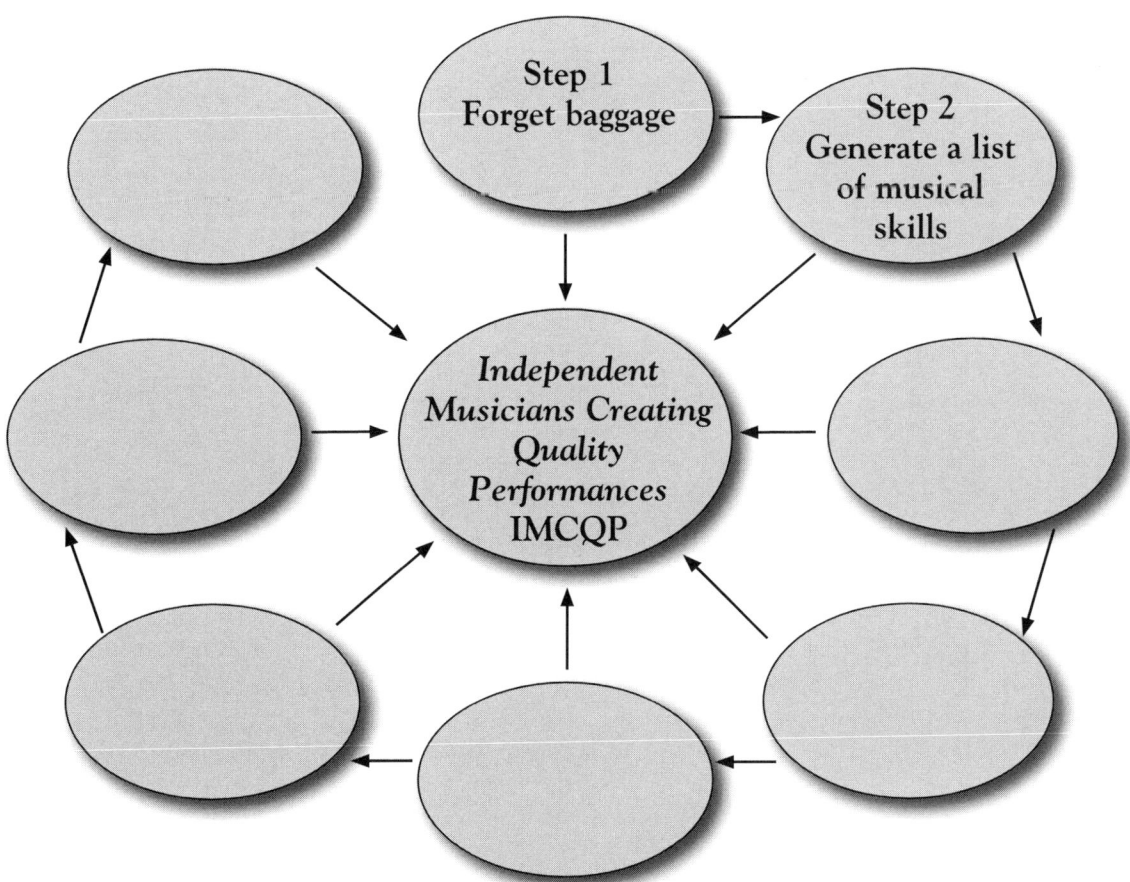

FIGURE 6.

CHAPTER 3
ALIGN MUSICAL SKILLS

This third step, aligning musical skills, allows the staff to discuss where and when skills should be introduced and when they will be tested. *Scale Your Way* is designed for the various types of school districts:

- Elementary School
- Middle School or Junior High
- High School
- K-12 School Districts

Think about what skills are needed for each grade level and the mastery level of those skills. Below are two of the eight *Basic Principles for Assessment for Learning* by Black & Wiliam that will help us clarify why we align skills.

MANAGING TEACHING AND LEARNING STYLES TO IMPROVE SKILLS AND PERFORMANCE

To think about the best set of strategies to use with your music students, begin by selecting from the thoughts below to build the best practices for your community of learners. Think about using a wide variety of activities within each lesson or unit of work. Choose some of these new suggested strategies to include in your planning for a lesson or unit of work. Remember that joint planning with a colleague increases the chance of success. These are generic and can be used across all curriculum areas and shared with your colleagues.

Visual/Spatial
- Mind maps
- Visual displays and opportunities for manipulating them
- Powerpoint presentations
- Flowcharts
- Use of color with purpose
- Concept maps
- Graphs, murals, montages

Auditory/Musical

- Listening to and creating audio tapes
- Using music at the beginning of a lesson to influence the learning environment
- Use rhythm to learn a key concept
- Put key words to a familiar tune
- Reading aloud key points; teacher exposition
- Create a concept song or rap

Kinesthetic

- Move around the room to collect information
- Model situations (e.g., raindrop water cycle march)
- Dramatization
- Move notes on cards around to find a sequence or rank order
- Lab experiments
- Charades and mimes
- Picture/information gallery

Interpersonal

- Group work
- Presentations and reporting back
- Discuss your plans/ideas/answers with a partner
- Role play
- Team challenges, for example problem solving
- Jigsaw approach where each member of the group finds out a different piece of information which they report back so that the group can put together the whole picture

Intrapersonal

- Individual work
- Diaries and logs
- Relating learning to personal experiences
- Personal target setting
- Silent work
- Autobiographical reporting
- Feelings and opportunities to empathize

Verbal/Linguistic

- Vocabulary quizzes
- Word games
- Group discussions
- Dart exercises
- Written reports
- Use mnemonics (e.g., Never Eat Shredded Wheat)
- Poetry writing
- Class debates

Logical/Mathematical

- Use flow charts
- Sequencing activities and timelines
- Use diagrams and lists
- Classify information
- Use statistics to find a pattern or reach a conclusion
- Predict: what will happen if...

Naturalistic

- Develop opportunities to do fieldwork or workout of doors
- Issues analysis (i.e., opportunities to question environmental issues and offer explanations)
- Research or exploration in the real world
- Opportunity to apply a strong sense of fairness in group work participation

Abstract Sequential

- Individual study
- Structured mental exercise
- Analysis and evaluation

Concrete Sequential

- Doing things step by step
- Maps and diagrams
- Tangible outcomes

Concrete Random

- Experiments/investigation
- Problem solving
- Big pictures not details

Abstract Random

- Group work
- Personalized work
- Discussion

BASIC PRINCIPLES FOR ASSESSMENT FOR LEARNING

According to *Inside the Black Box: Raising Standards through Classroom Assessment*, Paul Black and Dylan Wiliam encourage us to use the classroom assessment process and the continuous flow of information about student achievement it provides to advance—not merely track—student progress. The basic principles of assessment for learning are the following:

- Teachers understand and articulate in advance of teaching the achievement targets that their students are to hit.

- They inform their students about those learning goals in terms that students understand from the very beginning of the teaching and learning process.

These strategies nurture an open, honest, ethical, encouraging classroom assessment environment. As it plays out in the classroom, the impact of assessment for learning is that students remain confident that they can continue to learn at productive levels if they continue striving to learn. In short, the students don't fall victim to frustration or hopelessness because it is clear to the student and parent what skills and expectations are being taught, tested, and when the students should be able to demonstrate those skills. Empowering students to play a role in their own assessment allows them to monitor their own progress and take charge of their own learning.

Hinsdale South is a four-year independent high school district that is not a unit or K–12 district. As a result, our department needed to break skills into what would be taught from freshman to senior year and when the skills would be tested. It is important to differentiate between what is taught and what is tested. For example: Freshman may be taught a large amount of material such as intervals, scales, piano (for vocalists), or singing skills (instrumentalists). These may be taught but not tested in a large summative test or department final because it takes some time to master advanced skills such as interval recognitions aurally. Making and recognizing intervals is much quicker and totally within a student's ability in a freshman class. The students will be responsible for demonstrating (formative) that they can perform the advanced skill (making intervals and recognizing them on paper) but not tested to show mastery of the skill (hearing intervals and identifying them aurally) until the next year to allow for a logical maturation of skills. The students will be tested in quizzes or short tests on hearing and recognizing intervals in order to measure their progress but not tested for mastery on the large department semester finals in January and June.

Figure 7 presents a sample list of performance skills by year. A complete list of terms and performance skills is on the accompanying disc.

ALIGNING MUSICAL PERFORMANCE SKILLS WITH YEARS OF EXPERIENCE

Here is an example of first-year high school student performance requirements. Note that concerts are not listed, since we do not assess them formally.

- Perform individual solo at contest or in front of band for rating (required)
- Perform in a small group (ensemble) at contest for rating (required)
- Perform individual solo, scales, triads, and sightread (sing/play) in May (Jury)
- Perform scales (concert pitch): C, F, B♭, E♭, A♭, D♭, G♭, G (play); C, F, G (sing)

- Perform major, minor, diminished, and augmented triads on concert C, F, B♭, E♭, A♭, D♭, G♭, G (play); C, F, G (sing)
- Perform stepwise sightreading using solfège, note names, numbers, or syllables
- Sightread rhythms and rests (singing and playing [see list])
- Sightread in $\frac{4}{4}$, $\frac{3}{4}$, and $\frac{2}{4}$ (singing and playing)

From year to year, performances should show increased proficiency.

Skill or Term	Volume No.	Year Taught	Year Tested	Objective No.	Assessment Type					
1st and 2nd endings	1	1	1		W	L	IP	S	F	DF
1st inversion	3	1	2		W	L	IP	S	F	DF
2nd inversion	3	1	2		W	L	IP	S	F	DF
3rd inversion	3	2	3		W	L	IP	S	F	DF
8va		1	1		W	L	IP	S	F	DF
AB (binary) form	3	1	3		W	L	IP	S	F	DF
AB motive		1	3		W	L	IP	S	F	DF
AB ternary		1	3		W	L	IP	S	F	DF
ABA (ternary) form	3	1	3		W	L	IP	S	F	DF
ABA binary		2	3		W	L	IP	S	F	DF
ABA rondo		1	3		W	L	IP	S	F	DF
Accelerando	1	1	1		W	L	IP	S	F	DF
Accent	1	1	1		W	L	IP	S	F	DF
Accidental	1	1	1		W	L	IP	S	F	DF
Accompany	3	1	1		W	L	IP	S	F	DF
Adagio	1	1	1		W	L	IP	S	F	DF
Aeolian mode	3	1	2		W	L	IP	S	F	DF
D.C. al coda		1	1		W	L	IP	S	F	DF
Perform all ascending intervals (Major, Minor, Diminished, Augmented)		1	1		W	L	IP	S	F	DF

W • Written   L • Listening   IP • Individual Performance   S • Summative (Sum)

F • Formative   DF • Department Final

FIGURE 7.

TERMS AND PERFORMANCE SKILLS

SUMMARY

The completion of this third step of the eight in *Scale Your Way to Music Assessment* has allowed you to see the student's time with you as valuable and limited. You have focused your thoughts on Forgetting the Baggage, Generating a List of Musical Skills (SMU and SPS), and Aligning Musical Skills into a measured amount of teaching time. Said another way, when students will be taught and tested. You have begun to see that creating trained, educated, and independent musicians is a thoughtful process, not one of luck. Your students, parents, and administrators have no idea how fortunate they are to have teachers who understand what it takes to be a skilled educator who can create an environment for student success. Congratulate yourself on completing these three steps. You are well on your way to creating independent musicians.

We hope you will visit our website (www.mpae.net) and share with us and others how your musical journey is going. Let us congratulate you and give you feedback as you develop an assessment plan.

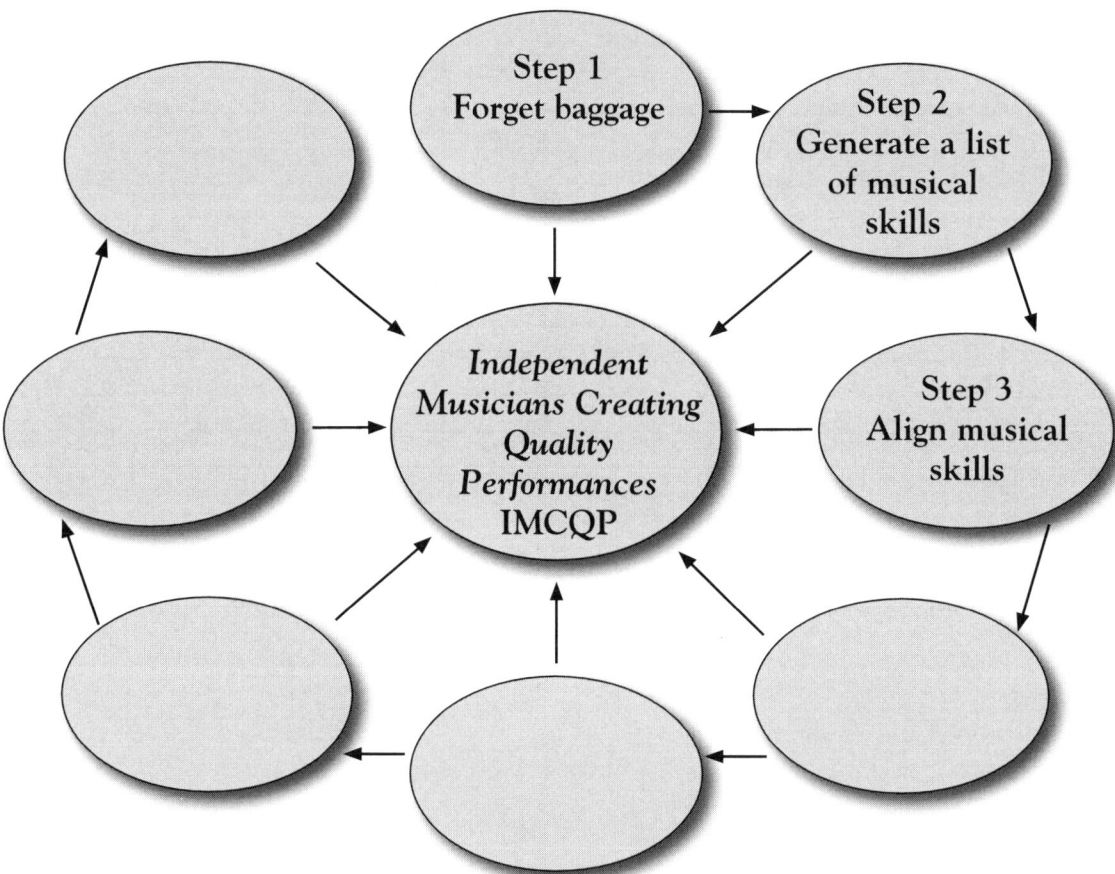

FIGURE 8.

CHAPTER 4
BUILD AN ASSESSMENT INVENTORY

Build a list of the assessment software in your school and what music software is available to purchase to create the assessments you want. Each school district is in a very different place in creating assessments. You will have to adjust your efforts depending on where your school is in the assessment processes.

This section is broken in two distinct sections:

- Test-making Programs
- Data Analysis Programs

It is essential for you to become familiar with the software that your school has to help you create quality tests or to assess test data. Most schools have someone in charge of the software and should be able to give you the information you need. If your school doesn't have such a person, then see the list of suggested software titles, companies, and websites in Appendix F to get you started. Several of the companies have samples for you to download, so be sure to check them out.

Don't invent everything. Start with music dealers and magazines for information on what is available. We have listed some excellent software for making tests and for assessing the data from those tests. Each year we review new software releases and compare them to what we currently use.

TEST-MAKING PROGRAMS

Alfred's Essentials of Music Theory 2.0

This program is divided into three volumes. Tests can be made by selecting pre-written questions or by writing custom questions. A workbook accompanies the software. If computers are not available, the material can be taught from the workbook. If a student misses a workbook session, she can review the missed material at a computer if available.

Once the material has been taught and tested, students who do not meet expectations can use the software to review the material in which they demonstrate weaknesses. The program tracks student progress, allowing teachers to check to see if remedial work was done and to check scores. We have found that setting a minimum score for advancement challenges students much as do the video games they play. Chapters 8 and 9 discuss using assessment software to break down test answers into usable data. For more information, visit www.alfred.com

Sibelius 4 and 5

Sibelius was originally a music composition software program that has turned into a very diverse teaching tool. The program allows you to create the music notation and text needed to create the aural portion of your tests or to write questions with examples in music notation. This feature allows you to assess a very important part of your curriculum as students apply their listening and note-reading skills on paper as well as select answers from music examples played.

A second, tremendously helpful aspect of the program is the worksheet feature. Sibelius comes with 1700 ready-made worksheets in addition to blank templates which allow you to add music notation to your questions. Appendixes A–E present examples of the types of questions you can create using the music notation software of your choice. Chapters 8 and 9 discuss using assessment software to break down test answers into usable data.

Educators who are short on money have several different options when purchasing, so be sure to examine the various versions available.

For more information, visit www.sibelius.com

Finale

Finale is a music composition software program that allows you to create the music notation and text needed to create the aural portion of your tests or to write questions with examples in music notation. This feature allows you to assess a very important part of your curriculum as students apply their listening and note-reading skills on paper as well as select answers from music examples played.

As with Sibelius, Finale comes with thousands of ready-made exercises and worksheets that can be customized to fit your specific situation. Appendixes A–E present examples of the types of questions you can create using the music notation software of your choice.

Chapters 8 and 9 discuss using assessment software to break down test answers into usable data.

Educators who are short on money have several different options when purchasing, so be sure to examine the various versions available.

For more information, visit www.finalemusic.com

Musition 3!

Musition 3! is a software-based music theory program. There is no workbook for in-class use.

As educators, we need to provide help for students who are not meeting expectations as well as advanced training for students wanting to develop a high level of proficiency in musical skills. Musition 3! is designed for students of all ages and abilities. It comes with hundreds of interactive tests that cover all levels from beginner to advanced, and are grouped into thirty-four topics.

The content can be customized to suit a specific class syllabus. Tests include multiple-choice questions or questions answered by clicking an onscreen piano keyboard. Custom tests can be created to suit your students' requirements. Student and class results can be printed in any of twenty-five useful reports, and marks are compiled over time so that student progress can be monitored from week to week.

For more information, visit www.sibelius.com

Auralia

Auralia is a software-based music theory program. There is no workbook for in-clase use.

As educators, we need to provide help for students who are not meeting expectations as well as advanced training for students wanting to develop a high level of proficiency in musical skills. Auralia is a great tool for teaching ear-training to students who are weak in this area. It is also beneficial for advanced students who want to develop their musical ear.

Auralia, with its numerous levels of difficulty, can be used in class and individually. It is an effective way to use technology to help develop music skills. Auralia emphasizes four domains: Intervals and Scales, Chords, Rhythm, and Pitch/Melody. Each of these areas is broken down into numerous sub-skills that are applicable to students in performance ensembles or advanced AP music theory classes.

For more information, visit www.sibelius.com

TEST ASSESSMENT SOFTWARE

Once you have developed and administered your tests, you will want to be able to look at results and discuss them with your staff. Numerous assessment software programs to help with these tasks are available. Here are several suggestions to consider. Be sure to talk to your administrators to see what they currently use.

Scantron has Part test-Par scores or Achievement series; Pearson has the Pearson Benchmark Assessment Series. Both of these are software programs with test-creating assessment facilities used by many of the school districts in the U. S. They are all-in-one solutions that provide everything needed, from making tests and test questions to aligning questions to state and national standrards and providing a database of questions for use in analyzing data gleaned from tests.

Both of these software programs can create either pencil-and-paper bubble tests or tests to be taken on a computer. At this time, neither program has the ability to add audio clips to questions, but in Chapter 9, we show you how to create those audio questions. Numerous school districts around the country are using these very powerful tools to keep track of student progress and analyze test data.

For more information, visit www.scantron.com and/or www.pearsonassessments.com

Microsoft Excel

Microsoft Excel can be used to calculate statistics with add-in software. Excel spreadsheets can also be imported into JMP, making it possible to use Excel for data entry and JMP for data analysis.

JMP

Pronounced "jump," this statistics software program can be used to explore data relationships to facilitate school improvement. JMP allows individual and group analysis of student performance scores.

It is hard to underestimate the value of its ability to distill performance data and subjective scores to numeric form, which can greatly facilitate the improvement of musical performance.

There is sample data from Microsoft Excel on the accompanying disc that you can import into JMP in order to evaluate the program. Chapters 8 and 9 present that data in graph form as generated by JMP. This shows how JMP data can be used to empower students and teachers to understand student achievement on performance skills, which enables students to learn and improve.

JMP is also valuable as a tool for planning classes and activities to help improve weaknesses in performance skills.

JMP is especially useful for exploring variables that affect student musical performance. For example, one variable that might have an impact on the level of musical performance is amount of practice time. So, in addition to assessing students' performance, you might also ask how much time they spend practicing each week. With JMP you can see the relationship between time spent practicing and the rating given to a student's performance. Not only can you see the total score, but you can also view the relationship between practice and each element of the performance. For example, you might find that those who practice more have better intonation than those who don't. This is just one example of how statistical software can help you better analyze assessment data.

We feel that the value of JMP cannot be overestimated, and so suggest downloading a free, thirty-day trial of the software at www.jmp.com

SPSS

SPSS is statistical software that creates graphs and charts from your data. If SPSS is available in your school, you can import the data on the accompanying disc and experiment with making graphs and charts. Chapter 9 presents examples of the types of reports and data analysis possible with this powerful statistical product.

For more information, visit www.spss.com

SUMMARY

You have now completed step 4 on your journey as you *Scale Your Way to Music Assessment*. As you read about the possible uses of software, you are likely to feel overwhelmed with information, new tools, and ideas.

Take the performance data on the accompanying disc, download a free trial of JMP, and begin to see the power of using performance assessment software. Visit the websites suggested; open your mind, considering how to use a music theory program in developing your students' understanding of music and your assessment writing.

Working with these tools will help your students, teachers, parents, and administrators see student achievement, not only on paper, but also in performance. Understanding where your students are in their musical development is essential in helping them achieve their full potential. Without unbiased information about our abilities, we would live in a world of little understanding of those abilities or our potential.

We hope you will visit our website (www.mpae.net) and share with us and others how your musical journey is going. Let us congratulate you and give you feedback as you develop an assessment plan.

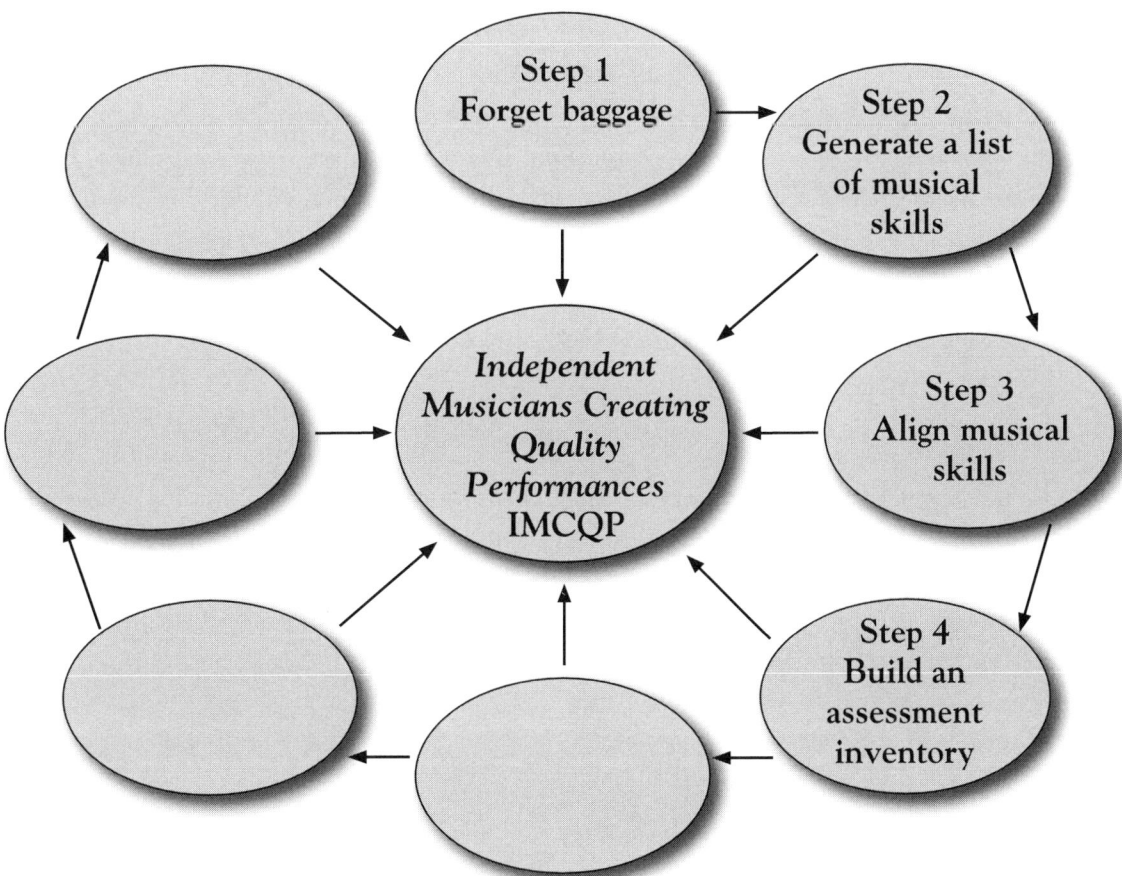

FIGURE 9.

CHAPTER 5
COLLECT DATA

It is important to collect data on what musicians are being asked to do outside of your school. Students in your programs will have the opportunity to participate in college auditions for scholarships, college performing groups, college music admission auditions, clinics, state district auditions, all-state auditions, and state solo and ensemble contests in addition to AP music theory courses. These are just a few of many opportunities in which your students could be involved. Preparing students for these experiences is part of our job as educators.

AUTHENTIC ASSESSMENT

Authentic assessment refers to assessment techniques that gather information about students' ability so that they can perform tasks found in real-world situations.

It is important to compare your department's list of skills with what outside groups are asking musicians to do. This will either validate your list or bring to your attention skills the outside musical world is asking of your students that your program is not teaching. The music skills that students are being asked to demonstrate in college auditions for performing groups, written music tests, and listening tests are a very good measure of what is going on in the real world in which we hope students will want to participate. Use these already-created standards to guide you in deciding what is best for your school and students.

Our school found that many of our students were not majoring in music, but were performing in college bands, orchestras, and choirs. After college, they were participating in church choirs, community bands, and theatre groups, which required them to perform, sightread, identify and sing or play intervals, chords, and major and minor scales. They also were taking written music theory tests to qualify to perform in groups for which they auditioned. With the information our students brought back from auditions we found that we were asking our students to do exactly what was being asked of them by colleges and universities. Our students not only left their auditions feeling confident about their performance, but ended up making the best groups because they were being taught with a real-world understanding of the outside world's expectations of musicians.

STATE AND NATIONAL STANDARDS

State and national organizations have spent years developing guidelines, standards, and lists of skills for music educators to use. Using this material is another way to connect what you do in the classroom with the standards outside experts recommend for schools. As a school in Illinois, it was important for us to teach what the Illinois Music Educators Association asked of our students at contest and district and state auditions. Don't write off state and national standards as unattainable, but do adjust them to fit your school. Visit the following websites and read what these organizations have to say:

www.ihsa.com
www.menc.com
www.imea.com

BEST PRACTICE

Best practice is what works best in peak-performing schools. These practices usually are supported by data to validate the practice in the field.

We have visited schools and talked to educators whenever possible, done research on educational trends, and are constantly looking for programs that set higher musical and educational goals. But we don't try to copy them, because there are too many variables in the reasons they do what they do. What we gain from seeing these programs is validation of what we are doing as a peak-performing school and making sure that our educational standards are not falling behind the outside world. It is important to take best practices and adjust them to the everyday situation in which we work. **Don't use your situation as an excuse to not do something. This takes you back to the baggage issue. Instead, adjust the best practice to your situation.** Don't be afraid to look at your program in relation to state and national standards and best practices. Open your mind to resources and ideas outside of your school and use them to improve your teaching and the musical skills of your teachers and students.

Including this information in everyday teaching, student performances, and theory requirements allows students to experience another reason to learn and apply music skills. In the larger context, we are making what we are teaching applicable to the outside musical world.

We don't have to look very far to find music theory and examples to teach, because they are in the music we play every day in rehearsal. The problem occurs when we play them without ensuring students understand the theory and make the connection between content and application.

SUMMARY

You have now completed five of the eight steps in *Scale Your Way to Music Assessment*. Having done this, you are now able to use the music you teach every day to teach the skills and vocabulary you believe the outside music world requires of all musicians. The skills you have selected and are teaching should be motivating and guiding your teaching.

Look at the music you are using in class. Does the musical information on the page scream to be learned and absorbed by your students? You and your students should be looking and listening to music with an understanding that comes from a blend of music theory and performance skills. This is why you love music and have chosen to educate others in this art. Young people are the future supporters and consumers of a very precious art form; they are our legacy for the future.

Use the list of music skills you have found in the outside world and have selected to teach to keep your rehearsals and lessons focused and goal oriented.

We encourage you to visit our website (www.mpae.net) and share with us and others how your musical journey is going. Let us congratulate you and give you feedback as you develop an assessment plan.

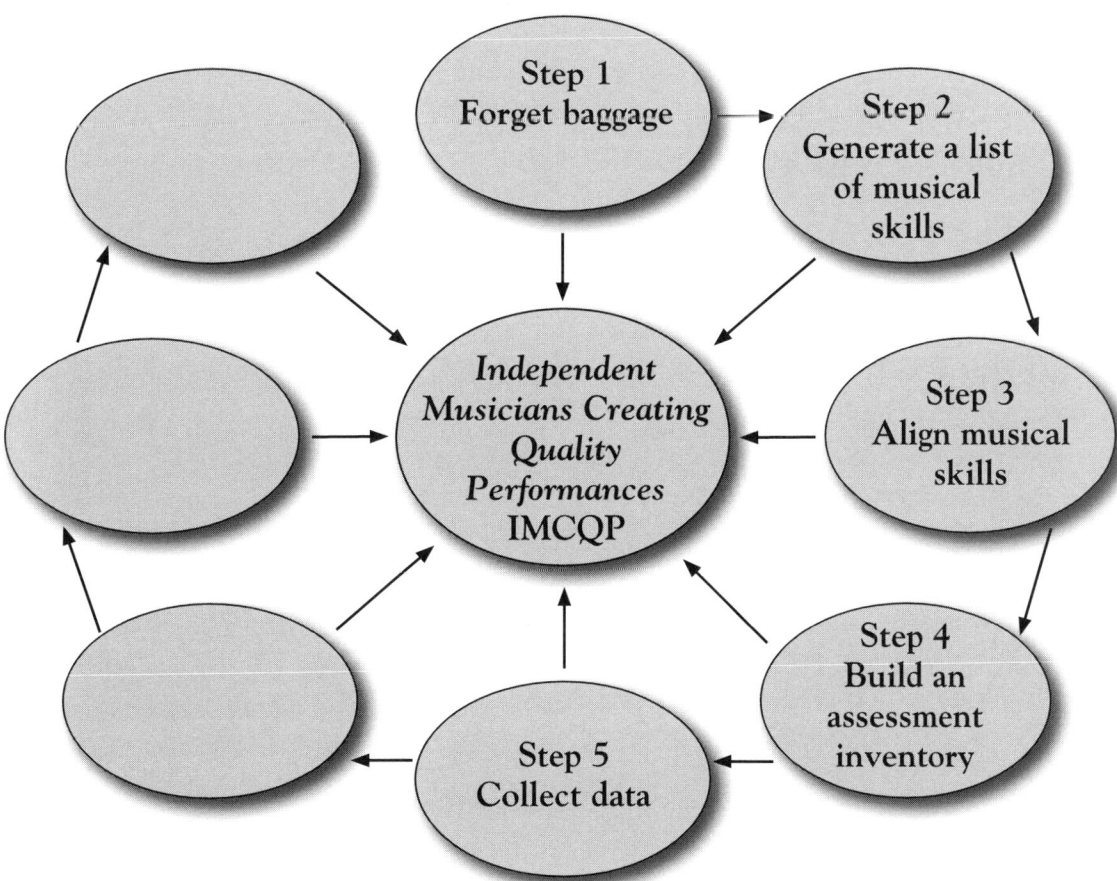

FIGURE 10.

CHAPTER 6
DEFINE GOALS

Define the existing goals of your school, department, and courses by reviewing and reflecting on their alignment with state and national organizations. If your music department does not have goals, begin developing them after reading this chapter.

On the next several pages you will see examples of how we connected our district goals to our department goals and how the department goals relate to state and national standards. Because this is a working document, we abbreviated with an (S) for state and an (N) for national standards followed by numeric standard for easy reference. You will see how we continued the process and wrote and connected department goals with course goals and national standards. Then we connected course goals with our objectives and assessments. Take some time to look over the examples in this chapter before reading on. This will help you understand how all of the goals and standards are related.

According to *Classroom Assessment for Student Learning: Doing It Right—Using It Well*, Stiggins, Arter, Chappuis, and Chappuis define goals in terms of Achievement Targets. An Achievement Target defines what your students need to know and be able to do to achieve success. The question we need to ask is: What do we want our music students to know and what music skills should they have to be successful in music? Achievement Targets vary by grade level. For example, we can't expect the same level of skill in sightreading from middle school as from high school students. Achievement Targets tend to be very broad at the school or district level and become very specific at the course level. In addition to defining Achievement Targets, we must also communicate these to students so that they understand what they need to know and do to be successful in music.

This crucial sixth step will guide your department and curriculum in the future. Let's break this section into four areas:

1. School and district goals
2. Music department goals and how they align with district goals
3. Course goals and how they align with department goals
4. Course objectives and how they align with course and state goals and your assessments

SCHOOL AND DISTRICT GOALS

Every school district should have goals for the total school population that guide the entire system. Get a copy and enter them in the template provided on the accompanying disc or use the template your school has. By completing this step, you will be able to show that what you are doing in your department and classroom is related to school and district goals.

Figure 11 presents the goals Hinsdale District 86 created. We have included these so you can see how district goals can guide the music department into creating goals.

MUSIC DEPARTMENT	DISTRICT EDUCATIONAL GOALS	We will acquire, construct, and apply knowledge.	We will identify and explore the connections between past and present, theory and application, individual and society.	We will solve problems, make thoughtful decisions, and evaluate processes and outcomes.	We will communicate in a variety of modes with clarity, meaning, and purpose.	We will appreciate the significance of both continuity and change.	We will develop and practice positive personal and social responsibilities.	We will build a passion for life-long learning.
PROGRAM/DEPARTMENT GOALS								

FIGURE 11.

MUSIC DEPARTMENT GOALS AND HOW THEY ALIGN WITH DISTRICT GOALS

Music goals must be related to national standards (MENC) and your state standards and goals. The National Association for Music Education (MENC) has spent years developing standards that should guide development of your department's goals. National standards and your state standards and goals will get your department talking and thinking about goals. Use these as a starting point and reference for writing your own goals. In addition to guiding writing for your program, national and state standards will validate your goals and demonstrate to your administration, teachers, students, and parents that what you are asking your students to do is in line with state and national standards.

For further clarity on the national standards and state standards/goals go to the following websites:

- National Standards: www.menc.com
- State Standards and goals for all states: www.education-world.com/standards/state/index.shtml

We have listed the national standards and our Illinois state goals so you can see how department goals mesh with them.

PART 1

It is a good idea to have national and state standards before you when meeting or working on department goals. If your department already has goals, check to see if they are in line with national and state standards and goals. If they are, enter them into the template on the accompanying disc and mark the boxes under district goals that match your department goals.

NATIONAL STANDARDS FOR MUSIC EDUCATION

Here are the standards set by The National Association for Music Education taken from the National Standards for Music Education. The complete National Music Standards and additional materials relating to them are available from The National Association for Music Education, 1806 Robert Fulton Drive, Reston, VA 20191.

1. Singing, alone and with others, a varied repertoire of music
2. Performing on instruments, alone and with others, a varied repertoire of music
3. Improvising melodies, variations, and accompaniments
4. Composing and arranging music within specified guidelines
5. Reading and notating music
6. Listening to, analyzing, and describing music
7. Evaluating music and music performances
8. Understanding relationships between music, the other arts, and disciplines outside the arts
9. Understanding music in relation to history and culture

ILLINOIS GOALS FOR FINE ARTS EDUCATION

State Goal 25: Know the language of the arts.
- Understand the sensory elements, organizational principles, and expressive qualities of the arts
- Understand the similarities, distinctions, and connections in and among the arts

State Goal 26: Through creating and performing, understand how works of art are produced
- Understand processes, traditional tools, and modern technologies used in the arts
- Apply skills and knowledge necessary to create and perform in one or more of the arts

State Goal 27: Understand the role of the arts in civilizations, past and present
- Analyze how the arts function in history, society, and everyday life
- Understand how the arts shape and reflect history, society, and everyday life

PART 2

When you are writing goals or Achievement Targets, you must first determine the type of target. For example, the target could be a knowledge, reasoning, or performance target, one in which you want students to produce a particular product to demonstrate proficiency, or one that targets attitudes or motivation. Once you have determined this, write your goal or Achievement Target to reflect this information. An Achievement Target consists of four essential elements:

- A description of the student
- A description of the behavior
- The conditions under which the behavior will be carried out
- The criteria for success

For example: *Tenth-grade vocal music students will demonstrate their ability to sightread by singing two pages from a song they have not practiced with a maximum of two errors.*

This particular objective is fairly specific and would probably be used at the classroom level. But it does contain all of the necessary elements. When this is shared with students they can see what they have to do and how well they have to do it to achieve success.

PART 3

Begin writing your department/program goals and entering them in the template provided on the accompanying disc. Note that we have marked on the template how our department goals correlate to the state and national standards. Here is one example of our goals.

Department Goal 3: *Students will understand and appreciate music theory and history through the music performed.*

Let us share with you how this goal came to be worded the way it is.

One of the steps our district took in getting department goals approved was to sit down with the school and district administration, outside consultants to our district, and our department chairs to read and explain our goals. The original wording was something to the effect of "Students will understand and appreciate music theory and music history." The superintendent reminded us that what you write is truly what you are going to be doing in the classroom, and that we must be able to show in our curriculum that we were doing that. He said, "So you are telling me that your teachers are teaching music history as a major emphasis of your department." We responded that this was true. He said again, "So you spend a large part of your teaching time teaching the history of music, and you can show me in your classes how you are teaching it and measuring it." We responded, "Well, we aren't teaching all of the music history for each period, but we are teaching the history behind each selection we perform." He chided: "Then say that, so your goal actually matches what you are doing."

This story demonstrates that having a goal on paper which doesn't truly state what is happening in the classroom could lead to problems. Teachers should not say things only so that they look good on paper; they need to make the paper statements a reality.

MUSIC DEPARTMENT		DISTRICT EDUCATIONAL GOALS	We will acquire, construct, and apply knowledge.	We will identify and explore the connections between past and present, theory and application, individual and society.	We will solve problems, make thoughtful decisions, and evaluate processes and outcomes.	We will communicate in a variety of modes with clarity, meaning, and purpose.	We will appreciate the significance of both continuity and change.	We will develop and practice positive personal and social responsibilities.	We will build a passion for life-long learning.
	PROGRAM/ DEPARTMENT GOALS								
MU 1	Students will understand and apply musical skills through performance. (S-25.4–26A.3d, 4d) (N-1, 2)		•		•			•	•
MU 2	Students will understand and apply music technology. (S-25.4) (N-4, 5, 7)		•		•				•
MU 3	Students will understand and appreciate music theory and history through the music performed. (S-25.A.4–25B, 26A–27.B.4a+b) (N-6, 7, 8)			•			•		•
MU 4	Students will be able to make connections between music and the other arts. (S-25.A.4– 25b.4+5) (N-7, 8, 9)			•	•	•			
MU 5	Students will understand how to rehearse and perform in a musical group. (S26.B.4c) (N-2, 7)		•	•	•	•		•	•

FIGURE 12.

WRITING COURSE GOALS AND ALIGNING THEM TO DEPARTMENT/PROGRAM GOALS

If your department already has course goals, enter them into the template on the accompanying disc and mark the boxes under the department goals that match your course goals. If you are writing department goals, they should be the same for all performance classes (band, varsity choir, orchestra, etc.). If you are wondering why these goals are the same for these different organizations, it is because they are all performance classes, and the course goals are broad enough that they really state the essence of what is happening in the performance-based classroom. These goals would not be the same for music appreciation, AP music theory, or beginning piano classes. Department goals would be the same for these, but not course goals. Remember these are goals, not objectives, so they should be broad and reflect what you are going to teach. Course goals should be related numerically to national and state standards and goals so that they have validity.

Figure 13 presents an example of a course goal and how it aligns to department, state, and national goals.

MUSIC DEPARTMENT	DEPARTMENT GOALS	Students will understand and apply musical skills through performance.	Students will understand and apply music technology.	Students will understand and appreciate music theory and history through the music performed.	Students will be able to make connections between music and the other arts.	Students will understand how to rehearse and perform in a musical group.
Course Code: 05610		MU 1	MU 2	MU 3	MU 4	MU 5
COURSE GOALS						
Develop musical performance skills on one or more instruments. (S26B.4c–26A.4d) (N-1, 2)		•				•
Understand concepts of pitch, timbre, and balance. (S26A.4c) (N-6)		•	•			•
Understand musical notation. (26A4d) (N-5)		•	•			
Understand basic elements of music theory and compositional form. (S25A.4–26A.4d) (N-4, 5, 6)		•	•	•		
Understand rehearsal responsibilities and relationships. (N-1, 2)		•				•
Understand the musical styles and history of music prepared and performed. (S27B.4A) (N-7, 8, 9)		•		•	•	
Develop critical and analytical listening skills. (S25.A.3+4+5–26.A.4c) (N-6, 7)		•	•			•

FIGURE 13.

WRITING COURSE OBJECTIVES AND HOW THEY ALIGN WITH STATE GOALS AND YOUR ASSESSMENTS

Writing course objectives and deciding how to assess them is perhaps the most exciting part of the process. This is the point at which you as the teacher get to decide how you will teach the larger goals. Figure 14 presents an example of one set of course objectives.

Objectives are really performance targets that are stated broadly at the district level and narrow as they funnel to the school, department, and classroom. All objectives need to specify the level and type of performance (written, playing, singing, etc.) that will be used to measure the objectives.

Course Alignment Template

COURSE GOALS	LEARNING OBJECTIVES		ASSESSMENT TASKS FOR OBJECTIVES					
		Students will...	F	S	F/S	DF	W	P
Goal 1 **Develop musical performance skills on one or more instruments** (S-26.A.4d–26.B.4c) (N-1, 2)	1a.	Demonstrate correct playing position, posture, breath support, and embouchure in performance situations	•				•	•
	1b.	Perform notated music, interpreting all symbols for pitch, rhythm, articulations, dynamics, and style			•	•		•
Goal 2 **Understand concepts of pitch, timbre, and balance** (S-26.A.4c) (N-5)	2a.	Perform with acceptable pitch, tone quality, and blend with other instruments			•	•		•
	2b.	Perform with dynamic balance appropriate to the piece of music, part being played, ensemble, and musical style			•			•
	2c.	Explain and demonstrate the relationship between balance and pitch	•					•
	2d.	Demonstrate the use of electronic tuning reference devices	•					•

F • Formative   S • Summative   F/S • Formative/Summative   DF • Department Final
W • Written Test   P • Performance

FIGURE 14.
MUSIC
SYMPHONIC AND CONCERT BAND

COURSE GOALS	LEARNING OBJECTIVES		ASSESSMENT TASKS FOR OBJECTIVES					
		Students will…	F	S	F/S	DF	W	P
Goal 3 **Understand musical notation** (S-26.A.4d) (N-5)	3a.	Demonstrate common musical terminology and symbols as seen on the printed page			•	•	•	•
	3b.	Demonstrate appropriate transposition for the student's instrument			•		•	•
	3c.	Perform notated music, interpreting all symbols for pitch, rhythm, articulations, dynamics, and style			•	•		•
Goal 4 **Understand basic elements of music theory and compositional form** (S-26.A.4d) (N-4, 5)	4a.	Demonstrate the construction of major and minor scales and key signatures			•		•	•
	4b.	Write and perform (sing/play/identify) major, minor, augmented, and diminished triads			•	•	•	•
	4c.	Perform major and minor interval relationships to the octave			•	•	•	•
	4d.	Write and perform a variety of meter signatures	•			•	•	•
	4e.	Recognize examples of fugue, rondo, march, and overture forms	•					
Goal 5 **Understand rehearsal responsibilities and relationships** (S-26.B.4c) (N-1, 2)	5a.	Perform musical selections following the gestures of a conductor as to meter, tempo, style, articulation, dynamics, and entrances	•					•
	5b.	Demonstrate appropriate care of musical instruments	•					•
	5c.	Independently prepare music for rehearsal and have it prepared at the appropriate time	•					•
	5d.	Demonstrate the appropriate role of the individual performer in an ensemble	•					•
	5e.	Demonstrate how to cooperate with each other in the rehearsal situation to create an appropriate atmosphere for learning	•					•
	5f.	Perform in a variety of settings, including solo performance, performance in a chamber group, and performance in a large ensemble	•					•
	5g.	Demonstrate ensemble tuning procedures with appropriate pitch control and balance	•					•

COURSE GOALS	LEARNING OBJECTIVES		ASSESSMENT TASKS FOR OBJECTIVES					
		Students will…	F	S	F/S	DF	W	P
Goal 6 **Understand the musical styles and history of music prepared and performed** (S-27.B.4.A) (N-7, 8, 9)	6a.	Write the history of the composer being performed	•				•	
	6b.	Perform and demonstrate appropriate performance styles of musical period being performed			•			•
	6c.	Write the historical background of the music being performed	•				•	
Goal 7 **Develop critical and analytical listening skills** (S-25.A.3 + 4 + 5–26.A.4c) (N-6, 7)	7a.	Identify errors in their performances and those of others, and demonstrate how to correct those errors	•				•	
	7b.	Compare and contrast their performances to those of others, and suggest ways to improve their own performances			•		•	
	7c.	Use recording equipment to record individual and group performances for critique	•					•

F • Formative   S • Summative   F/S • Formative/Summative   DF • Department Final
W • Written Test   P • Performance

SUMMARY

If you are doing more than just reading *Scale Your Way*, you have applied and completed step 6, giving you a document of which few music programs can boast. You can take these six levels of goals and objectives to your administration and show them that music is a thought-out and defined subject that is as valid as any core curriculum class. You have accounted for and aligned course objectives with department, district, state, and national goals. You can show on paper that what you are teaching has national, state, and local support. As you worked through this chapter , we hope you have begun to see how goals and objectives translate into tests and teaching strategies for you and your department.

We hope you will visit our website (www.mpae.net) and share with us and others how your musical journey is going. Let us congratulate you and give you feedback as you develop an assessment plan.

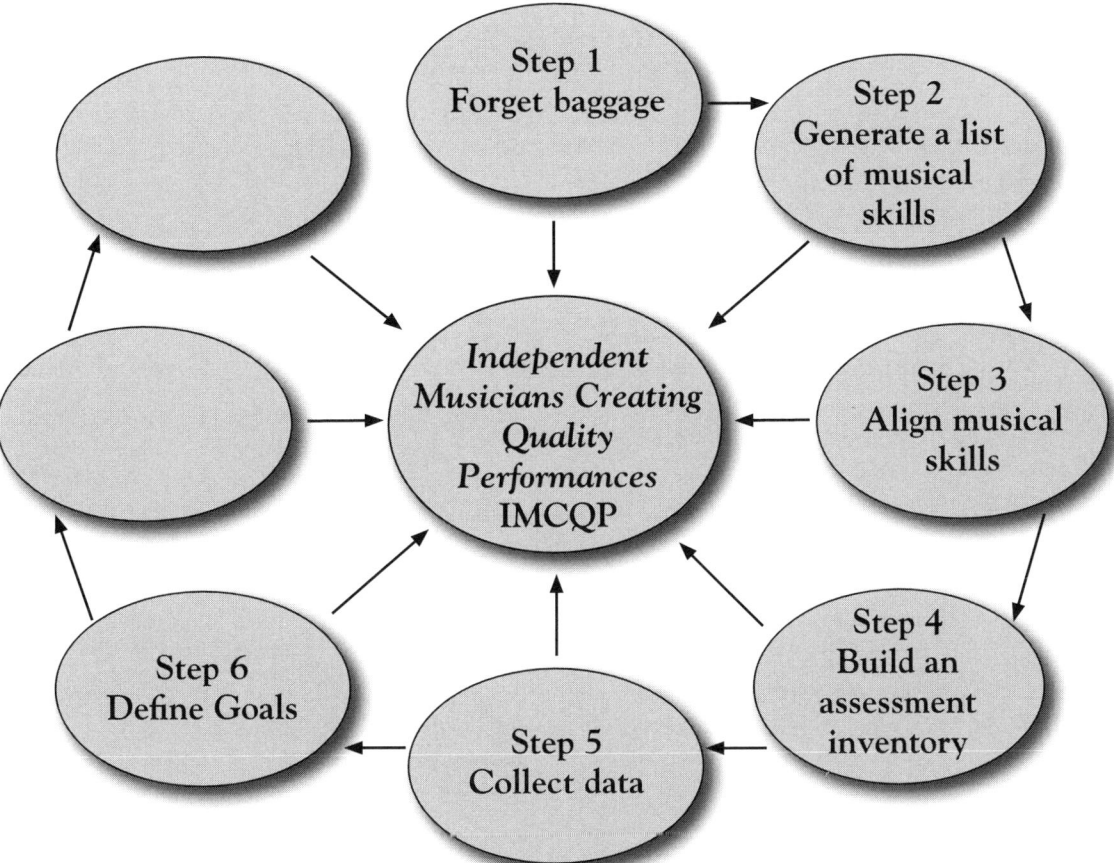

FIGURE 15.

CHAPTER 7
EMBRACE ASSESSMENT LITERACY

Embrace assessment literacy! The power of the word "embrace" clearly states how educators need to look at assessment and assessment literacy in schools and classrooms. Embracing means accepting and surrounding yourself with the knowledge of assessment and uses of data, and seeing the value of using assessment to improve teaching and student learning. In order to implement this seventh step correctly, you will need to immerse yourself in the power of assessment.

For the last twenty-three years, we have observed a change from a focus on group performances to one that looks at each student and her understanding of music and performance level through assessment and performance assessment. Teachers look forward to seeing results from written and listening tests broken into an item analysis by class, department, and individual student. We have developed an end-of-the-year jury performance for each grade so that teachers see the results of teaching or lack thereof in a measurable system. This has helped us to improve our teaching tremendously. We still take poor individual performances personally, but are able to understand where growth has occurred or not by looking at the total numeric picture of these performances. (This will be discussed further in Chapter 9.) But the most exciting result of our journey into assessment is seeing teachers use these results to improve their teaching, and students use those results to improve their skills and performances. This is why we assess: to improve ourselves and our student performers (Independent Musicians Creating Quality Performances—IMCQP).

For a moment, let's take a wider view of assessment and let Del Harnisch and other assessment experts speak to what assessment literacy means to education. We have put together in the next few pages adaptations of articles and handouts by Rick Stiggins, Judy Arter, Jan Chappuis, and Steve Chappuis from ETS Assessment Training Institute, Inc., Portland, Oregon. We thank them for their permission to share these adaptations.

ASSESSMENT AND SCHOOL IMPROVEMENT

According to *Inside the Black Box: Raising Standards through Classroom Assessment*, Paul Black and Dylan Wiliam believe that improving local assessment systems has become a major focus of school improvement efforts because states are requiring local assessment system planning and because improving local assessment systems can have a dramatic effect on student motivation and achievement. So educators are coming to assessment from two places: mandates and felt needs. Regardless of the motivation, educators need sound plans based on a vision of what a high quality, instructionally relevant assessment system looks like and on an understanding of how to put it in place. They also need training and professional support to implement these plans.

HELPING A PROGRAM REALIZE ITS VISION

Leadership is essential for reaching school improvement goals. Each leader of an academic program should create a vision of the benefits of assessment and how to make that vision a reality. How best to do this depends on context and the support for an overall school improvement effort. What follows are important elements to consider in building the rationale for development of a teaching community that is assessment literate.

ASSESSMENT LITERACY DEVELOPMENT

The goal is to develop a balanced assessment system at the local level—that is, a system that combines large-scale standardized tests and day-to-day classroom assessments in ways that maximize student success.

Lorrie A. Shepard states in "Interview on Assessment Issues" that, over the past fifty years, we have witnessed the growth of a very strong standardized testing tradition in American schools. In recent years, we've even witnessed intensification in the belief that large-scale, once-a-year tests pave the path to effective schools. Policymakers at all levels believe that holding schools accountable for producing high test scores will compel educators and students to work harder and smarter. As a result, they believe, students will learn more and schools will be more effective.

These tests do serve valuable purposes. They provide evidence of student achievement that is comparable across classrooms, schools and districts. They inform once-a-year resource allocation, program planning and policy setting decisions. Clearly, if standardized tests are of high quality, and if assessment users understand the meaning and limitations of the resulting scores, then sound decisions can be made and schools and students can benefit.

Unfortunately, test scores that arrive once a year cannot provide a sufficient assessment basis for the development of effective schools. The reason is that they often arrive too late in the year to be used to make changes in teaching and learning. It's not that they are inappropriate—indeed they are very appropriate; it's that they are insufficient. Standardized assessments are only one source of assessment data and simply provide a means to compare classrooms or schools. While this is helpful, when used alone it is not an effective means to further school improvement. The key to real school improvement, according to *Classroom Assessment for Student Learning: Doing It Right—Using It Well* (Stiggins, Arter, Chappuis, and Chappuis), lies with the classroom teacher who continuously collects data in the classroom and uses that data to make strategic changes in teaching methods and curriculum content.

Large-scale, standardized assessments can't assess all the important learning outcomes we have for students—for example, oral presentations and interactions with peers. Such information has to be gathered at the classroom level. In addition, there are many standards that cannot be sampled sufficiently by large-scale assessment; assessment of these standards needs to be supplemented by assessment information collected at the classroom level. Examples are writing selections, mathematics problem solving, reading, designing scientific experiments, and most importantly to us, music performances.

In order for teachers to make the instructional decisions necessary to maximize student achievement, they need to continuously and accurately monitor this achievement. It's not enough to wait until the end-of-the-year standardized test results are available to see how it went. Teachers, students, and parents, all of whose decisions drive school quality, don't make decisions once a year. They make them throughout every school day, with strategic evidence from their classrooms providing the basis for instructional decisions. In *Student-Involved Assessment for Learning* (Richard J. Stiggins, 4th ed.), this is called Assessment for Learning. Much of what you see in the examples in *Scale Your Way* reflects how a music program leader has chosen to make this a reality.

Thus, just as large-scale, standardized assessments must be of high quality to produce accurate information for decision making by administrators, so must those assessments designed by teachers for their own day-to-day decision making. If classroom assessments are of high quality, produce accurate information, and are effectively used, students can prosper.

This is precisely why balanced assessment systems are so crucial to the development of effective schools. Different people need different information about student achievement at different times and in different forms to do their jobs. Both standardized and classroom assessments must be of sound quality for schools to be effective.

While we can generally count on standardized tests to be of high quality, we can't count on them to be understood, and we can't count on classroom assessments to produce dependable and accurate information about student achievement. Few states require competence in assessment as a condition to be licensed to teach or become a principal. So, with some notable exceptions, colleges of education simply haven't provided the training teachers and administrators need to do their assessment jobs. It has been so for decades. As a result, we remain a national faculty unschooled in the principles of sound assessment. In general, educators do not have the assessment skills needed to generate accurate information for classroom decision making.

Therefore, to achieve balance, fulfill our assessment responsibilities, and meet current mandates for assessment that increases student learning, we need to invest in bringing the classroom assessment side of the equation into the school improvement process. We need to provide teachers and principals with the assessment literacy needed to do their jobs. Teachers need to understand the differences between sound and unsound assessments so they can make their essential contributions to student success.

Three concrete and specific benefits will accrue as the result of this investment in assessment literacy and in balancing assessments: greater student desire to learn, markedly higher levels of achievement, and the development of life-long learners.

MOTIVATION LINKAGES TO IMPROVED STUDENT LEARNING

The responsibility for improving student learning does not just lie with teachers. Involving students in the classroom processes of assessment development, recordkeeping, and communication seems to bring about a fundamental shift in their internal sense of responsibility for academic success. By improving the quality and effectiveness of use of classroom assessments, we can help teachers raise the confidence of their students and tap a whole new wellspring of energy for learning.

Greater motivation yields higher achievement. A comprehensive international literature review and analysis conducted by Paul Black and Dylan Wiliams of Kings University in London and reported in the November 1998 *Phi Delta Kappan* reveals almost unprecedented jumps in student achievement attributable to improved quality of classroom assessment. Further, these researchers go into great detail about the role student-involved assessment, recordkeeping, and communication played in increasing achievement. There can be no question: students learn more when their teachers are assessment literate.

By bringing student-involved classroom assessment online in our school improvement efforts, we set students up to become life-long learners. To illustrate, students who cannot (a) monitor the quality of their own writing and fix the text when it isn't working or (b) monitor their own reading comprehension and change strategies when they aren't getting it, cannot become independently functioning life-long writers or readers. Self-assessment of the quality of one's own writing or reading comprehension lies at the very heart of what we define as literacy. Those who can't do it are not competent.

By involving students in the classroom assessment process, we put them in touch with the tools needed to check and fix their own writing, reading, music performance, and more. By involving students in assessment, we bring them to a place where they don't need us anymore to tell them that they have done well. In effect, we teach ourselves out of a job. We submit that this is precisely what we are paid to do.

For all these reasons—balance, general lack of understanding of sound assessment, the role of accurate classroom information in producing standards-based schools, and the role of student-involvement in increasing student achievement—we began by improving the assessment literacy of educators in our district through the application of very specific professional development and planning mechanisms.

PLANNING FOR SUCCESS IN SCHOOL IMPROVEMENT

To realize improved student performances, we propose developing a balanced, instructionally relevant local assessment system through two sets of actions: conducting professional development in classroom assessment and planning, and implementing a local infrastructure that supports and encourages a balance of large-scale and classroom assessment for the benefit of students. Each of these sets of actions is described below. The third part of the plan for success describes a plan for evaluating program impact.

PROFESSIONAL DEVELOPMENT IN ASSESSMENT LITERACY

We propose improving the assessment literacy of our teachers and administrators through learning and team-based professional development using materials developed for that purpose by the Assessment Training Institute. One text that can form the foundation for this teacher-centered learning program is *Student-Involved Classroom Assessment for Learning* (Richard J. Stiggins, 4th ed., 2005).

RATIONALE FOR A LEARNING TEAM APPROACH TO PROFESSIONAL DEVELOPMENT

Practice with Student-Involved Classroom Assessment (Judith A. Arter and Kathleen U. Busick, 2001) repeatedly cites the use of collaborative group work and learning as the most powerful mechanism for developing the "professional learning communities" needed to support ongoing school improvement. Change requires doing things differently in the classroom. Additionally, "For teachers to be successful in constructing new roles they need opportunities to participate in a professional community that discusses new teacher materials and strategies and that supports the risk-taking and struggle entailed in transforming practice" (Putnam and Borko in *Practice*). In fact, in several studies, teachers cite the opportunity to collaborate as the most important factor in instituting change. There is also research evidence that learning in groups significantly improves learning and that, although structures for group work vary widely, all are more effective than learning alone.

Workshops by themselves can provide small doses of information in an effective and efficient fashion. Experts can sift through the information that participants need to know and offer motivational sessions to energize a faculty into wanting to learn more. But taken alone, workshops cannot provide the practice with feedback needed to implement new ideas in the classroom. Individual study by itself allows the learner to tailor information gathering to one's own needs, practice with ideas in an applied setting, and proceed at one's own pace. But taken alone, individual study can be inefficient and doesn't allow practice with feedback, bouncing ideas off of others, or other support during the learning process. Learning teams provide structure for learning about a complex topic, flexibility in structure and pacing, colleagues with whom to learn, and a support system for practice. In learning teams, participants share lessons learned in the classroom and learn from each other.

How does this apply to learning about classroom assessment? We are used to thinking about assessment as the measurer of change—the index of what students have learned through various instructional innovations. But a more powerful approach is to view classroom assessment as the change itself—a direct precipitator of learning; a way to significantly alter the relationships between teachers and students in ways that promote student learning to higher standards. Because of the complexity of what is to be learned about classroom assessment, we must approach professional development on classroom assessment the same way as other topics—through classroom-contextualized learning teams.

In a learning team, a small group of educators agrees to meet regularly to take joint responsibility for their collective development. Between meetings, each team member agrees to complete an assignment designed to advance his own assessment literacy. Those assignments provide instruction on new strategies, an opportunity to experiment with new ideas in the classroom, and focused reflection on the results. The result is a series of powerful learning experiences.

STANDARDS-DRIVEN SCHOOLS

A learning team perspective is important in standards-driven schools because of its implications for both high- and low-achieving students. When perennially high-achieving students are confronted with much higher standards and expectations than those to which they have been accustomed, their history of success often gives them enough confidence to turn up the energy, learn more, learn faster, and meet the higher standards. Their prospects of continued success are good, they know it, and they respond accordingly. Success becomes its own reward. Throughout their lives, the awareness and assumption of success has provided these students with the inner reserves of confidence they need to risk trying to learn more. This response to self-reflection yields more success, more confidence and more willingness to take risks. The "upward spiral" of a success-oriented student is described in *Making the Grade: A Self-Worth Perspective on Motivation and School Reform* (Martin V. Covington).

Not all students approach high-stakes tests with the same optimism. For some students, the spiral can go in the other direction. Their personal academic histories lead them to believe that meeting world class standards is not attainable. Their academic histories, characterized by chronic failure, do not allow the expectation of success. These students often regard success as beyond their reach and capacity. For them, challenge holds only the prospect of even more public evidence of failure. They are most likely to respond by withdrawing from the fight and giving in to hopelessness. Covington describes these learners as "failure accepters."

In short, the motivational effect of high standards and high-stakes tests is not the same for all students. For some, it represents more cause for optimism; for others, it represents just another occasion for defeat and hopelessness. Some students learn and continue to grow while others suffer and drop out. There are opposite responses to the same assessment.

Current researchers in classroom assessment have learned to find ways to encourage high- and mid-range achievers to grow even faster, while at the same time preventing low achievers from giving up. Research conducted in the United States and around the globe reveals that the way to maximize learning is not to maximize anxiety, but to maximize students' belief that they can and will learn if they keep trying (see Crooks, 1988; Black & Wiliam, 1998; Harnisch et al., 2006). Additionally, in *Learned Optimism: How to Change Your Mind and Your Life*, Martin E. Seligman states that he believes we must redefine the relationship between assessment and student motivation as one in which we use assessment to build each student's sense of academic optimism, not to build the confidence of some and destroy that of others. Another way to understand the key elements to school improvement are the Five Doors as described in *Assessment for Learning: An Action Guide for School Leaders* (Stephen Chappuis, Ricchard Stiggins, Judith Arter, and Jan Chappuis). Take a few minutes and look at the doors below to get a better understanding of how to think of school improvement, not just in music, but in your building.

DOOR 1
CLEAR ACHIEVEMENT TARGETS

- Teachers and administrators must know and understand achievement expectations
- Curriculum directors and faculty must have a general vision of how success is realized in the local curriculum
- Teachers must be prepared to succeed

DOOR 2
SERVE ALL ASSESSMENT USERS

- Focus assessment on individual students rather than large numbers of students
- Use multiple assessments to meet needs
- Plan carefully for assessment use
- Understand what information is needed

DOOR 3
DEVELOP ASSESSMENT LITERACY

- Key attributes
    - Know what to assess
    - Know why you are assessing
    - Know how you are assessing
    - Know what assessment evidence you need
    - Know how to assess accurately
- Quality standards
    - Clearly specified and appropriate targets
    - Assessments designed for specific purposes
    - Assessment methods reflect intended targets
    - Provide representative sample that permits confident conclusions
    - Develop assessments that eliminate bias and distortion
- Barriers to accurate assessment
    - Personal barrier: emotions
    - Institutional barrier: lack of time
    - Community barrier: community beliefs
    - Ultimate barrier: lack of assessment literacy
- Removing barriers
    - Understand differences between sound and unsound practices
    - Commit to meeting quality standards
    - Apply principles of assessment for learning

DOOR 4
COMMUNICATING EFFECTIVELY

- Sender and receiver must understand achievement expectations
- Assessment information must be accurate
- Receivers must be open to hearing and understanding assessment information
- Schools should take advantage of information management systems

DOOR 5
CREATING A SUPPORTIVE POLICY

- Prepare school boards and communities for sound assessment
- Develop an assessment-literate school staff
- Rethink school policies
  - Curriculum
  - Grading
  - Homework
  - Graduation requirements
  - Communicating assessment information

SUMMARY

Congratulations! You have finished step seven of the eight steps needed to implement sound assessment practices in your program and school. Understanding and embracing assessment is a major step in your assessment journey. By taking on this task, you have driven the performance arts to a new level in your school and have joined forces with those who understand how assessment fosters learning in students and teachers. While the process of producing high-quality assessments seems like a lot of work, the reward of producing musicians who can give high-quality performances and have the skills to do well in college auditions is worth the effort. We spend much time and energy teaching students how to perform well, and, as we listen to them, we can hear the fruits of our labors. In addition, just as we point out areas in our students' performances that need improvement, we should also be willing to look at our own work and ask, "What can I improve?" When we ask this question and design assessments to generate data that will help us to improve those areas, the result is better performances by our students. Although learning to design high-quality assessments to improve teaching and learning is a new area for many, the benefits to your school and especially your students will be worth it.

We hope you will visit our website (www.mpae.net) and share with us and others how your journey is going. Let us congratulate you and give you feedback as you develop an assessment plan.

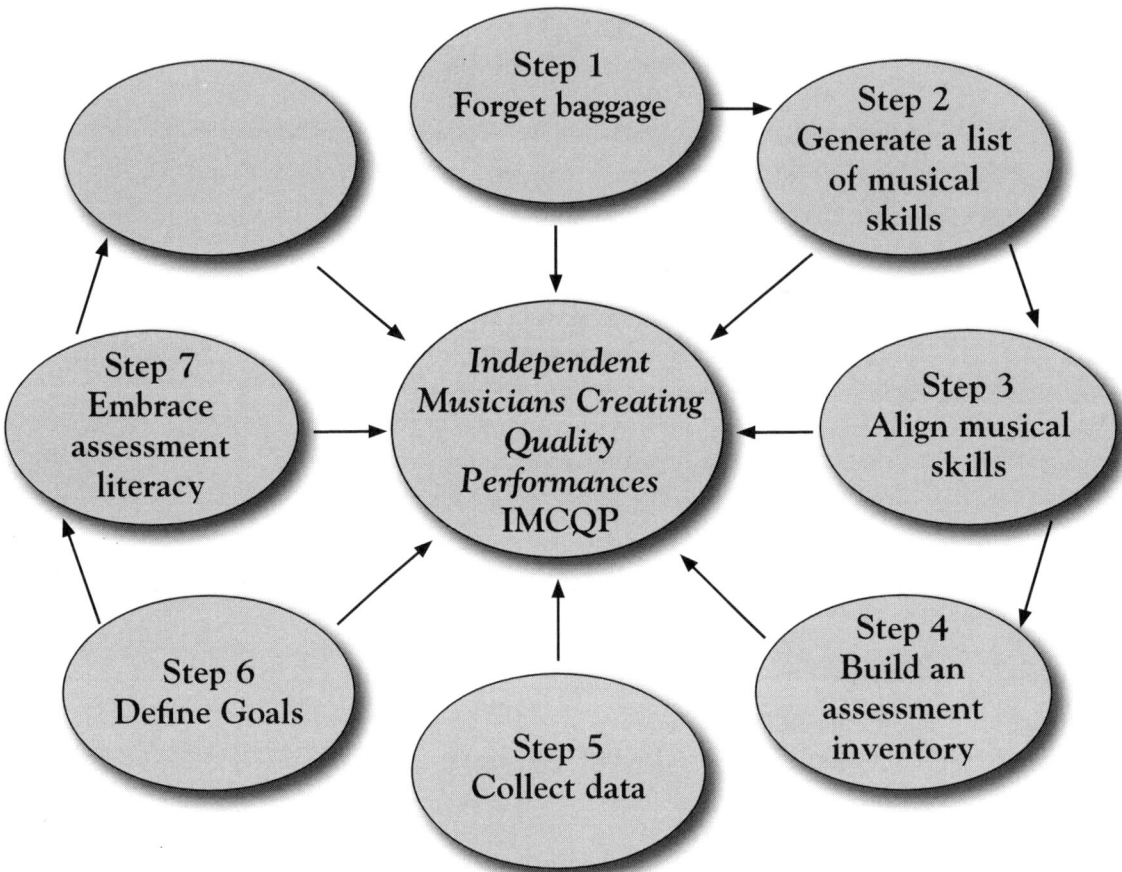

FIGURE 16.

CHAPTER 8
FORMULATE ASSESSMENTS

Developing assessments should be an essential part of your music program. In the arts, educators need to assess three types of learning goals for students, as described in previous chapters: performance, music theory, and listening. These can easily be assessed using four assessment methods: selected response, short answer, extended written response and performance assessment. On the pages that follow, we provide ideas on how to use:

1. performance assessment to assess musicianship
2. selected response and short answer to assess (subsets of theory and listening)
3. extended written response to assess (a subset of theory and listening)

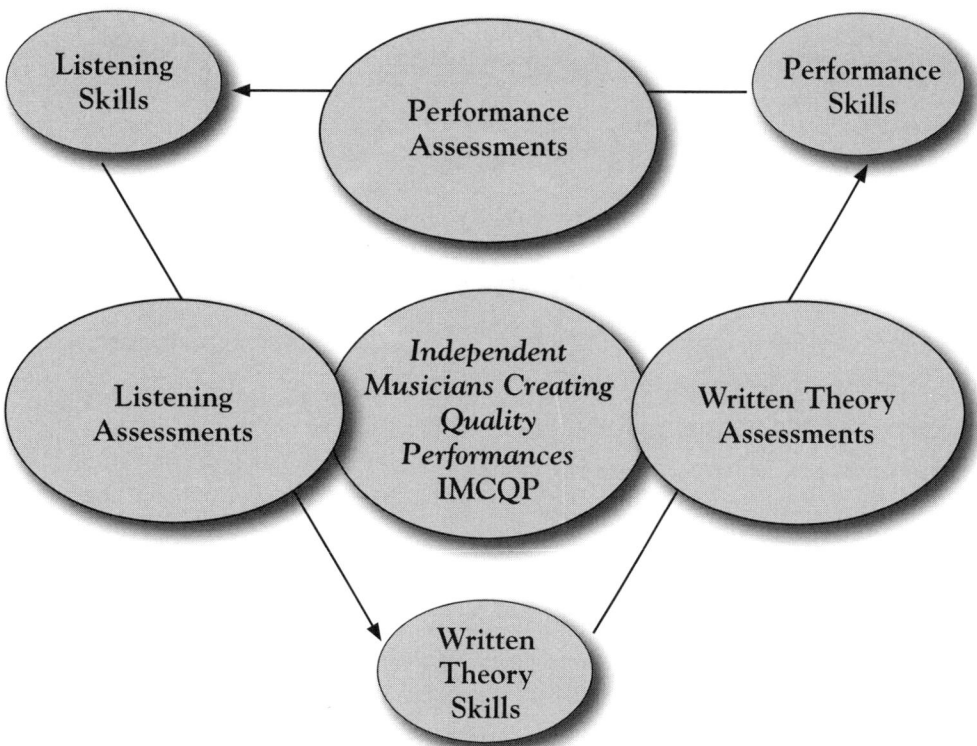

FIGURE 17.

Performance assessment is the assessment of students as they engage in an activity. It is an on-the-spot evaluation of performance, behavior, or interaction. There is no concrete product that can be judged at a later stage, unless it is an audio or videotape record of the original performance.

Curriculum documents include many learning outcomes which describe process, activities, or performances. These outcomes can be broadly characterized as "performances." To assess performance outcomes, students must be observed in action.

Performance assessment can be thought of as a "purpose" continuum, as shown in Figure 18, with classroom formative and diagnostic assessment at one end and high-stakes summative assessment at the other. Informal classroom observations are to the left of the continuum; teachers' planned classroom assessment events (e.g., a teacher/student music check-off of parts, or a group playing/singing sections together) are in the center of the continuum; and externally set high-stakes assessments, such as a solo or ensemble performance at contest or an end-of-the-year jury performance are to the right.

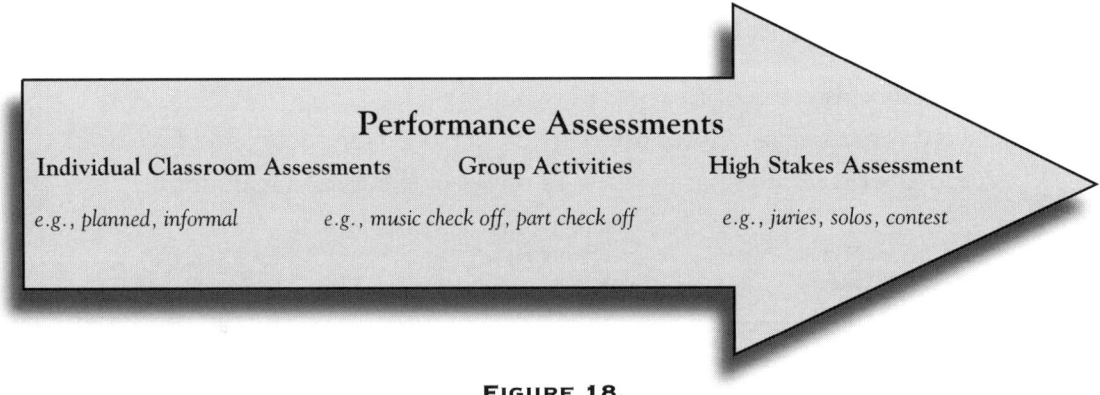

Performance Assessments

| Individual Classroom Assessments | Group Activities | High Stakes Assessment |
| e.g., planned, informal | e.g., music check off, part check off | e.g., juries, solos, contest |

FIGURE 18.

PLANNING PERFORMANCE ASSESSMENTS

The usefulness of evidence provided by performance assessments for inferring a student's level of achievement depends on:
- Relevance and coverage (a validity issue)
- Amount of evidence (a reliability issue)

RELEVANCE AND COVERAGE

Relevance describes the degree to which the evidence addresses knowledge, skills, and understandings (or outcomes) of the learning area. Classroom teachers are likely to be interested in ensuring that observations of student performances focus on instructional goals and that there is a match between planned performance tasks and outcomes to be assessed.

Coverage describes the degree to which evidence samples the range of outcomes in a learning area. Music education teachers usually observe a variety of student performances in an attempt to collect evidence about a range of their skills. Teachers are also likely to be interested in developing ways to efficiently record anecdotal information about student performances in order to provide systematic evidence that can guide instruction and provide feedback to students and parents.

AMOUNT OF EVIDENCE

Although assessments of student achievement are based on specific tasks, the purpose and interest is always in the knowledge, skills, and understanding required to perform those tasks. The intention is to infer a student's achievement in an area of learning from their performance on specific tasks, that is, to generalize from a limited performance sample.

This observation raises the question of the amount of evidence (number of tasks) required to provide a sufficiently accurate estimate of a student's general level of achievement. This is particularly important in high-stakes contexts in which student performances influence all-state music selection, chair placement, grades, and admission to music schools, scholarships and recognition awards.

FOR DISCUSSION

An assessment that asks students to perform an interesting or complex activity is not necessarily a good assessment. Good assessment reliably measures something beyond the specific tasks that students are asked to complete. The results of good assessment identify what students can do in a broad domain of knowledge or skill. The skills that students exhibit in an assessment situation should transfer to other situations and problems.

Before beginning to develop performance assessments, answer the following questions:

- What music skills should students at each grade level be able to demonstrate? (Look at the list you have made and what years you have assigned for each skill.)

- What type of performances will be required of each student in order to demonstrate these skills?

- How do these skills help to create independent musicians who can prepare music without help?

You have already done much of this work by creating a list of skills and objectives and marking those you plan to test in writing or performance. Now the task is to order them into specific tests.

CREATE ASSESSMENTS THAT
Encourage, not discourage
Build confidence, not anxiety
Bring hope, not hopelessness
Offer success, not frustration
Trigger smiles, not tears

Classroom Assessment for Student Learning: Doing It Right—
Using It Well (Stiggins, Arter, J. Chappuis, and S. Chappuis)

FIGURE 19.

What assessments might you conduct next week that
your students wouldn't want to miss?

Arts educators need three types of assessments:

1. individual performance assessments to assess musicianship
2. selected response and short-answer questions to assess theory skills
3. selected response and short-answer questions to assess listening skills

Although these assessment types are interrelated, we will focus on how to develop individual performance assessments first.

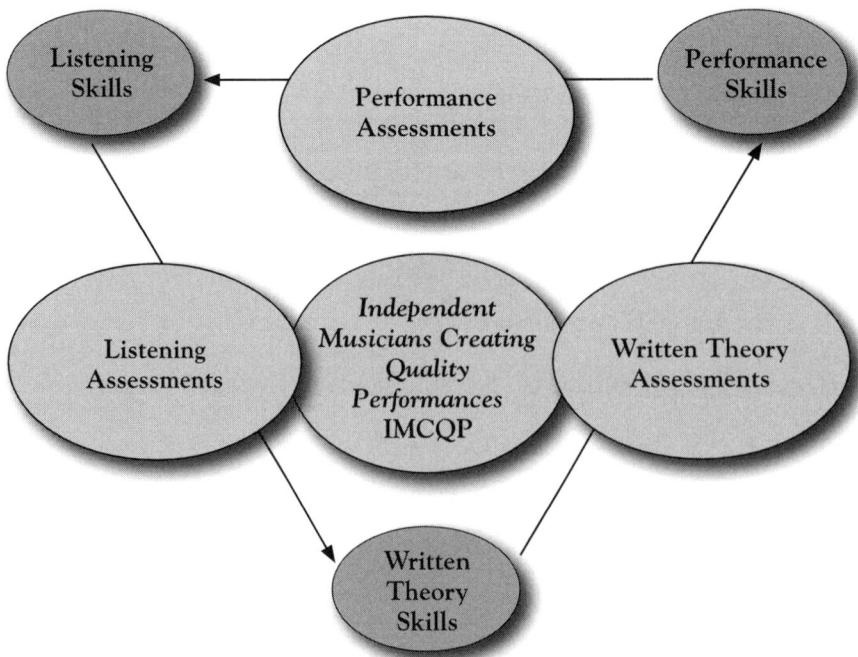

FIGURE 20.

PART 1: DEVELOPING PERFORMANCE ASSESSMENTS

In order to assess a performance, rubrics or guidelines must be created for teachers and students to follow when listening to, performing, or judging music. Originally, we first tried to create rubrics using words like "meets" or "exceeds," but we found these descriptors confusing and difficult to use. We wanted a simple, clear format that students, teachers, and parents could understand. We selected a rubric that seemed to meet those criteria on one of the music adjudication forms from the National Federation of State High School Associations (NFHS) used by the Illinois High School Association at state contests. There are eleven music adjudication forms free to download from the NFHS website (http://www.nfhs.org/web/2004/02/ music_adjudication_forms.aspx). Forms are available for:

Solo
Large Group
Swing/Show/Jazz Choir
Small Ensemble
Instrumental Jazz Ensemble
Piano-harp Solo/Ensembles
Marching Band (1-Part)
Marching Band (4-Part) Marching and Maneuvering - General Effect
Marching Band (4-Part) Marching and Maneuvering - Execution
Marching Band (4-Part) Marching and Maneuvering - Music Execution
Marching Band (4-Part) Music General Effect

These forms are in Microsoft Word format and can be edited for your specific needs. The document format and musical terms are clear and consistent. We suggest that you consider using the vocabulary on the forms in your daily rehearsals.

These forms reference five performance levels:

Superior	Outstanding in nearly every detail
Excellent	Minor defects
Good	Lacking finesse and/or interpretation
Fair	Basic weaknesses
Poor	Unsatisfactory

Areas of concern assessed are:

Tone Quality	resonance, control, clarity, focus, consistency, warmth
Intonation	accuracy to printed pitches
Rhythm	accuracy of note and rest values, duration, pulse, steadiness, correctness of meters
Technique	(facility/accuracy) artistry, attacks, releases, control of ranges, musical and/or mechanical skill
Interpretation, Musicianship	style, phrasing, tempo, dynamics, emotional involvement
Diction	vocal
Bowing	strings
Articulation	winds
Other Performance Factors	choice of literature, appropriate appearance, poise, posture, general conduct, mannerisms, facial expression (vocal), memory (if required)
Sightreading, Scales	

Figure 21 displays a copy of the NFHS form for soloists.

PART 2: TEACHING STUDENTS AND TEACHERS: HOW TO JUDGE A SUBJECTIVE ART

Teaching students how to judge a subjective art like music is one of our main goals as educators. Students need to be able to understand and discriminate between what is considered acceptable musical technique and what is not. In order to do so, students must listen to performance examples of individuals (solo) and ensembles to develop an inner aural library of sounds. Can you imagine trying to learn to speak French correctly never having heard the language spoken? Educators can not expect students to recreate quality musical sounds if they have not developed an aural base from which to draw. Students must learn that people who hear their music will base their opinion on a standard they have developed by listening to the best soloists and ensembles available. Subjectivity in music comes from listeners making judgments based on what they like and what they have heard. A person with a limited listening background will make a less-educated evaluation of a person's musical ability. Ways to develop your students' aural library without impacting your rehearsal time are suggested below. Your rehearsal time won't be affected, but your rehearsal quality will be. Developing your students' aural library will create better rehearsals, because students will understand the type of sound you are asking them to replicate. Let's take a look at how to judge performances and what the literature has to say.

NFHS MUSIC ADJUDICATION FORM
SOLO

Order of Appearance: Click & Add   Date: Click & Add   Program/Event No.: Click & Add
Event: Click & Add   Class: Click & Add
(tenor solo, trumpet solo, etc.)

School Name: Click & Add   Location-Contest/Festival: Click & Add
Name of Soloist: Click & Add

Selections	Composer	Publisher
1.		
2.		
3.		

Place one of these numbers in each box below, then total carefully.
5 — A superior performance — outstanding in nearly every detail.   2 — A fair performance — basic weaknesses.
4 — An excellent performance — minor defects.   1 — A poor performance — unsatisfactory.
3 — A good performance — lacking finesse and/or interpretation.

AREAS OF CONCERN	COMMENTS
Tone Quality Consider: resonance, control, clarity, focus, consistency, warmth	
Intonation Consider: accuracy to printed pitches	
Rhythm Consider: accuracy of note and rest values, duration, pulse, steadiness, correctness of meters	
Technique (facility/accuracy) Consider: artistry, attacks, releases, control of ranges, musical and/or mechanical skill	
Interpretation, Musicianship Consider: style, phrasing, tempo, dynamics, emotional involvement	
Diction - Vocal **Bowing - Strings** **Articulation - Winds**	
Other Performance Factors Consider: Choice of literature, appropriate appearance, poise, posture, general conduct, mannerisms, facial expression (vocal), memory (if required)	
Sight-Reading, Scales	

TOTAL POINTS

_____
(signature of adjudicator)

Divisional Rating _____

RATING COMPUTATION TABLE

Without Sight-Reading		With Sight-Reading
35-32 points =	Division I (Superior)	= 40-36 points
31-25 points =	Division II Excellent)	= 35-28 points
24-18 points =	Division III (Good)	= 27-20 points
17-11 points =	Division IV (Fair)	= 19-12 points
10-7 points =	Division V (Poor)	= 11-8 points

NFHS
PO Box 690
Indianapolis, IN 46206
Phone: 317-972-6900; Fax:317.822.5700
www.nfhs.org

FIGURE 21.

JUDGING PERFORMANCES

When performances are judged in order to infer a student's level of achievement, two features of the assessment need to be considered:

- the method of judgment
- the comparability of judgments (inter-rater reliability)

METHOD OF JUDGMENT

Performances are judged either analytically or holistically. Teachers make an analytic judgment of a student's performance when they rate different aspects of the performance. Teachers make a holistic judgment of student's performance when they give it a single rating based on their overall impression of that performance.

A dance performance, for example, might be rated for content and performance features—ideas, organization, pace of delivery, volume, facial expression, and audience engagement. Teachers may report these ratings separately (analytically) or use them to make a final assessment of the performance at the bottom of the national form (holistically).

COMPARABILITY OF JUDGMENTS

A fundamental feature of performance assessment is its reliance on judgment. Two people viewing the same performance can judge that performance differently. To ensure that assessments are fair, that is, that the rating of a student's performance does not depend on who assesses it, it is important to minimize differences among assessors. This is called inter-rater reliability. In the classroom context, whether another teacher would make the same judgment of a student's performance using the same marking guide (rubric) is not usually of great concern. In high-stakes contexts (jury performances), however, inter-rater reliability is crucial. Here are some other areas where judges are trained to judge subjective subjects.

In large-scale exams where hundreds and thousands of students take AP Exams as well as state and national writing exams such as ACT and SAT, judges are brought together before they grade the exams. They discuss levels of expectations, rubrics, and what represents the standard everyone is expected to use, so that all judges are using the same criteria to grade students' work. Subjectivity can be reduced if the standard is clear to the judges and everyone agrees on the level for each numeric score. We have all experienced a judging situation where one judge gave all high ratings while another gave all low ratings. How frustrating to be subjected to inconsistent judging. This is why you must train your judges before they listen to jury performances.

Usually, the greater the requirements for comparability of performance assessments, the more precisely the assessment criteria are specified. In a high-stakes situation, such as district or state music contests, the criteria for assessment may be tightly specified. Judges may be trained with the marking process then carefully monitored to ensure a high level of inter-rater agreement. (See below for data on judge reliability.)

DEVELOPING STUDENT SKILLS

Start each rehearsal with two to three minutes of a recording of a solo. Select a different instrument each day; take one minute to comment on the performance using terms from the national assessment rubric. After several days of modeling comments about the performance, allow students to make comments, and encourage use of the rubric vocabulary terms.

In addition to solo recordings, play recordings of the type of group you are teaching. For example, a band director might play a recording of the Eastman Wind Ensemble or the University of Illinois bands. When rehearsing a transcription from orchestral literature, it would be good to play the orchestral version and comment on what techniques the orchestra uses and how a band is asked to duplicate those sounds on wind instruments. This gives students an aural library to which they can refer when asked to duplicate a sound.

The next phase in developing a student's aural library is to make a video demonstration of each performance level: Superior, Excellent, Good, Fair, and Poor. We recorded a student teacher playing an etude and singing an art song at each performance level. Students found this very entertaining. But more importantly, they remembered the examples of the levels and could apply them to their own playing and their critique of other performances.

Another strategy can be used in warm-ups. Ask students to hold up the number of fingers that represents their rating of another student's or the group's tone. Everyone can raise fingers together (even including the teacher), allowing you to quickly discuss the tone quality. This activity is a formative assessment and gives both teacher and student immediate insight into the students' understanding of the various levels on the national form.

When implemented in a rehearsal, all of these activities create students who understand the performance standards that are expected in the classroom as well as in the outside world. This helps students articulate what they should expect from themselves. These strategies alone, however, will not develop the musical skills necessary for quality musical performance. Teachers must provide students with exercises and musical training that will develop those skills.

PART 3: ASSESSING INDIVIDUAL PERFORMANCE

The next part is to ask the students to record and rate themselves according to national performance standards. This recording will allow them to hear what they actually sound like and then comment on the performance, just as teachers and judges will do. Model this activity with the entire class before the individual rating. The group should listen to a recording of a student performance and fill out a form together before rating the recording each made of his own solo to better understand the musical terms to be used. This encourages students to take ownership of developing listening and performance skills outside of the classroom as they complete this activity on their own.

PART 4: PROVIDING REAL LIFE EXPERIENCES

It is important for students to learn that in the real world they will be judged quickly and subjectively, not only in music, but in other life situations where performance counts, such as interviews, projects, and presentations. Students must also learn to take criticism and reflect on performances and comments from others. Likewise, it is important for the teacher to learn how to hear someone else's comments about one of their student's performances without taking them personally. We must be able to accept outside judgments or criticisms if we hope to improve student learning and our own teaching. Reflection after a contest is a powerful learning tool. When students perform for judges who have no prior expectation and receive a score on that one performance, that snapshot of their abilities can be used to enhance their overall musical skills.

PART 5: CREATING A JURY OR FINAL PERFORMANCE FOR EACH GRADE

The end of the year should be a time for all music students to demonstrate and celebrate the skills and abilities they have learned. Having students perform an individual solo or etude in addition to scales and triads in front of a panel (jury style) allows the staff and judges to evaluate the students in a culminating event or a summative assessment. In addition to your staff, the panel of judges should include two or three outside musicians who have never heard the students. Having outside judges allows the teacher to stay objective about what students can do. Each judge listens to performances and rates students using the national adjudication form that students have used all year. Scores are then added together to give students and staff an accurate score for categories listed on the rubric sheet. Scores can be analyzed using JMP statistical software for the entire department or by individual groups (choir, band, and orchestra) in order to see what skills are improving or still need to be developed. These data allow teachers to improve classroom instruction.

PART 6: USING ASSESSMENT TO IMPROVE CLASSROOM INSTRUCTION

This is why we assess: to use information from individual performances to improve student skill level. This data should be used to improve instruction and drive what and how we teach. When the staff hears each individual perform, a discussion is possible about what students understand and are able to do with the skills being taught. The next several pages illustrate how we used students scores from contest and the end-of-year jury performance (adjudicated by five to six judges) to track student and department growth in the eight areas listed on the performance rubric above. JMP, the statistical software discussed earlier, was used to create charts and graphs showing growth in each area. A complete set of data is given in Chapter 9.

A blank template and sample data for you to use to get started are on the accompanying disc. Take a few minutes to study these, noting column headings and the data provided. Having these things in mind can help you understand the value of assessment data as you read the next section.

Figure 22 presents scores for one band, one vocal, and one orchestra student taken from a Microsoft Excel spreadsheet.

SPECIAL NOTE

Data entered in Excel will not be formatted as in Figure 22; it will be in one row for each student. Figure 22 is formatted differently to make it easier to compare judges' scoring. The data is from senior performances only.

	State Contest Judge	May Jury Judge 1	May Jury Judge 2	May Jury Judge 3	May Jury Judge 4	May Jury Judge 5	Average
Band Student							
Tone Quality	4	3.5	3.5	4	4	4	3.83
Intonation	5	4	4	4	5	3	4.16
Rhythm	5	4	4	4.5	3.5	5	4.33
Technique	5	4	4	4	4.5	4	4.25
Interpretation/ musicianship	5	3	3	3.5	4.5	3	3.66
Diction/bowing/ articulation	5	4	4	4	4	4	4.16
Performance factors	5	4	4	5	5	5	4.66
Scales/Triads	5	4	4	5	4	5	4.5
Vocal Student							
Tone Quality	3	3	3	3	3	3	3
Intonation	3.5	3	3	3	3.5	3	3.16
Rhythm	3.5	4	4	3	3.5	4.5	3.75
Technique	3	3	3	3	3	3	3
Interpretation/ musicianship	3	3	3	2	3	3	2.83
Diction/bowing/ articulation	4	3	3	3	4	5	3.66
Performance factors	4	3.5	3.5	3.5	4	4	3.75
Scales/Triads	4	5	5	3.5	4	3	4.08
Orchestra Student							
Tone Quality	5	3	3	2.5	3	3	3.25
Intonation	4	4	4	2.5	3.5	4	3.66
Rhythm	5	3.5	3.5	2	3	4	3.5
Technique	5	3	3	3	3	3	3.33
Interpretation/ musicianship	4	3	3	2	3.5	3	3.08
Diction/bowing/ articulation	5	3.5	3.5	3	3.5	4	3.75
Performance factors	3	4	4	3	4	5	3.83
Scales/Triads	5	3.5	3.5	2	2.5	3	3.25

FIGURE 22.

SENIOR BAND, VOCAL, ORCHESTRA LIVE PERFORMANCE RATINGS

JMP

Figure 23 presents senior performance ratings data in graphic form. Performance criteria are on the vertical axis; scoring is on the horizontal axis. This graph is called a box plot. Box plots give more information than standard bar graphs. Let's use the features of box plots to describe our data.

Look at the Rhythm row in Figure 23. There is a horizontal line with vertical lines (known as whiskers) at each end and a gray box in between these lines. The box encompasses 50% of the ratings, from the 25th to the 75th percentile—in this example, from a rating of approximately 3.5 to 4.5. The other 50% of the ratings fall outside of the box. The vertical black line inside the box marks the 50th percentile, or the median—a rating of approximately 4.0 for Rhythm. The whiskers (vertical lines at the end of the horizontal line) mark the lowest and highest ratings for Rhythm.

For Rhythm, the lowest rating is about 2.5, while the highest is about 4.4. Look at the ends of the Rhythm, Tone Control, and Intonation rows, you will see three small O's. These denote values that are outside of the rest of the data, or ratings that are not representative of the group. The formal names for these values are outliers. It is permissible to delete outliers when calculating the average for a group, because they are not representative of the group. For example, some student musicians may have received bad ratings because they were ill and performed at a much lower level than usual. This is why multiple sets of data are needed to determine a student's true ability.

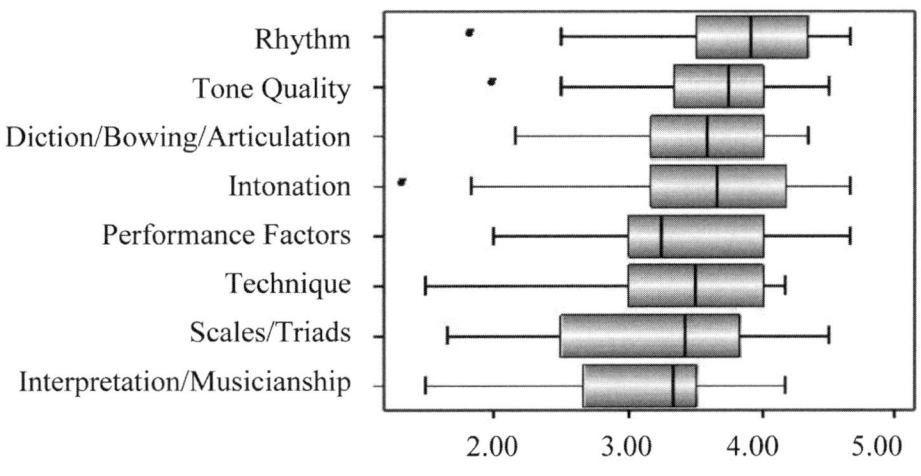

FIGURE 23.

YEAR 1: ALL EIGHT CRITERIA

Displaying numerical data in graph form makes it easy for your staff to visualize student achievement in each of the eight areas and discuss ways to improve student scores. Figures 22 and 23 show senior data for Year 1. This data is even more powerful if all five years of scores for seniors are compared.

Figure 24 shows five years of senior data for scales and triads. The Year 1 column shows that students were not performing required scales and triads at an acceptable skill level. After discussing the data, our staff decided to incorporate the scales and triads into rehearsals to reinforce them. Columns for Years 2–5 show that by doing this students' scale and triad skill level in live performance increased.

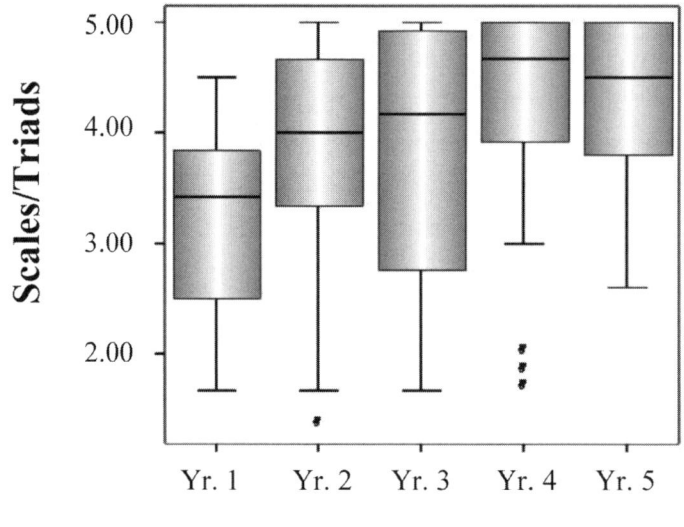

FIGURE 24.

SENIOR JURY AND MARCH SOLO CONTEST ACROSS FIVE YEARS

HOW DO WE KNOW THAT INDIVIDUALS JUDGING SCORES ARE RELIABLE?

JMP can also give a coefficient Alpha—a statistic that indicates data reliability. Coefficient Alpha measures the degree of consistency in rating between judges. The higher the Alpha, the more consistently the judges rated a performance, meaning that the data is more reliable. If only one judge rated a performance, a parent or student could say the judge's evaluation was subjective, or perhaps that the judge "didn't like them." This is why multiple judges are employed—it makes subjectivity harder to prove. Coefficient alpha quantifies judge consistency.

Figure 25 is an inter-rater reliability table based on the scales and triads data for Years 1–5 given in Figure 24.

Note that the Alpha is 0.92. The highest possible value for Alpha is 1.0. In this case, 0.92 indicates a very high internal consistency in the judges' ratings.

We hope that music educators will become leaders in performance assessment and use what is learned to improve instruction. Seeing student performance data is powerful for both students and teachers. How to use such data is discussed in Chapter 9. All of this data serves our commitment to developing independent musicians who are well educated in performance, theory, and music appreciation—our primary goal.

		JUDGE 1	JUDGE 2	JUDGE 3	JUDGE 4	JUDGE 5
JUDGE 1	Pearson Correlation	1	0.699*	0.625*	0.701*	0.650*
	N	140	140	140	118	84
JUDGE 2	Pearson Correlation	.699*	1	0.715*	0.800*	.638*
	N	140	140	140	118	84
JUDGE 3	Pearson Correlation	0.625*	.715*	1	0.658*	0.743*
	N	140	140	140	118	84
JUDGE 4	Pearson Correlation	0.701*	0.800*	0.658*	1	0.713*
	N	118	118	118	118	84
JUDGE 5	Pearson Correlation	0.650*	0.638*	0.743*	.713*	1
	N	84	84	84	84	84

* $p < 0.01$ for level of significance on correlations

Assumes absence of People*Rater interaction.

Reliability coefficients
     N of Cases = 84.0   N of Items = 5

Alpha = 0.9209

FIGURE 25.

INTER-RATER CORRELATIONS AND RELIABILITY OF RATINGS

TIPS ON DEVELOPING PERFORMANCE ASSESSMENTS

Performance in music should be assessed using a rubric (Stiggins, 2005). The NFHS music adjudication form is an example of a rubric that is used for high-stakes assessment. Rubrics can also be developed to assess performance in the classroom or with ensembles. A simple rubric consists of the criteria to be evaluated and an evaluation scale. Your rubric should incorporate the criteria used in adjudicating state competitions as well as skills that students will be expected to demonstrate in auditions for college music programs and music groups. Rubrics are often written in the form of a matrix with the performance criteria in the first column on the left side and the evaluation scale listed across the first row. In addition, there is usually a point value that is assigned to each category in the evaluation scale.

The criteria for evaluation that are used in the rubric flow out of the learning targets that you have established. For example, if you have a learning target regarding vocal performance, evaluating criteria should be related to the target objective as well as criteria that others agree are essential elements of a good vocal performance.

As you adevelop your rubric, you should establish guidelines about what constitutes differences in ratings for each of the criteria. For example, suppose you are rating intonation, defined on the state adjudication form as accuracy to printed pitches. What separates a rating of 4, meaning excellent (only minor defects) from 3, meaning good (lacking finesse and or interpretation)? When possible, it is good to describe what is lacking. Begin by writing a description of the highest level of performance in each area. In the case of vocal performance, such a description would include each criterion on the form such as intonation, tone quality, and so on. These all get a rating of 5. Next, go to the opposite end of the scale and describe the characteristics of the lowest level of performance for each criterion.

	Rating 1	Rating 2	Rating 3	Rating 4
Criterion 1	1.0 (pv)	3.0 (pv)	1.0 (pv)	3.0 (pv)
Criterion 2	1.5 (pv)	1.5 (pv)	2.5 (pv)	1.5 (pv)
Criterion 3	2.5 (pv)	1.0 (pv)	1.5 (pv)	1.0 (pv)
Criterion 4	1.0 (pv)	2.0 (pv)	2.5 (pv)	1.0 (pv)
Criterion 5	3.0 (pv)	2.5 (pv)	1.0 (pv)	2.0 (pv)

pv = point value

FIGURE 26.

A SAMPLE RUBRIC IN MATRIX FORM

Once this is complete, go back to the highest level and determine what would be missing to give the performer a rating of 4 in each area. Do this for each of the remaining areas. One advantage of including written descriptions for each criterion is that outside raters will be quickly able to see what you are looking for. Another advantage is that if you give this to students preparing for a performance, they will quickly see what your expectations are and will be able to better prepare. This is not an easy task. It takes collaboration among faculty and outside colleagues.

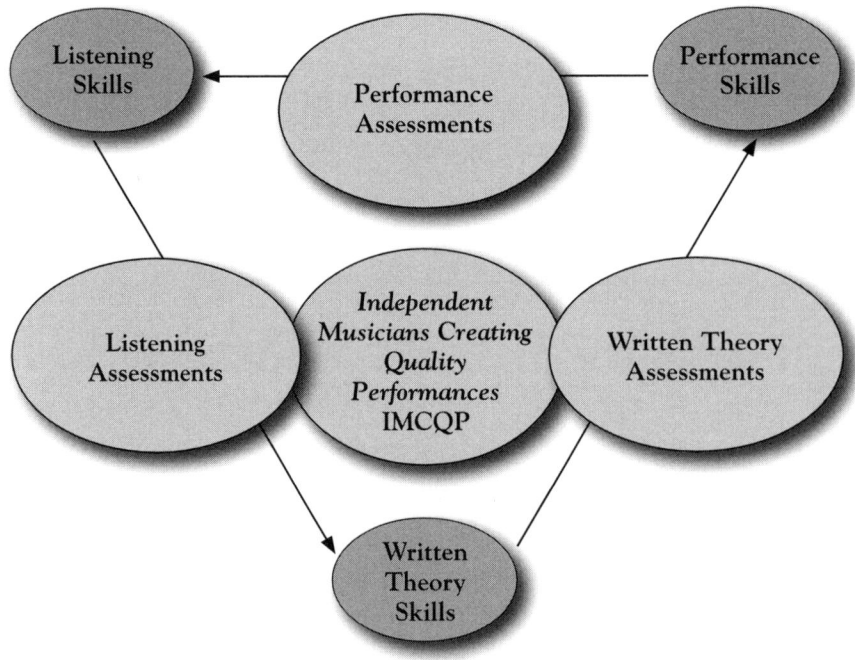

FIGURE 27.

HOW TO DEVELOP WRITTEN ASSESSMENTS

In order to develop high-quality written assessments, first seek examples of tests and questions in order to establish a baseline of understanding. You can build on what you learn from them to establish a standard for writing assessments. Some software programs come with templates for written assessments, or even finished tests you can use or adapt. We suggest you review the AP Music Theory tests at www.apmusictheory.com as well as the test-making capabilities of current theory programs to help you in developing written assessments.

Go back to your list of skills and objectives and note those you want to test in written and listening format. Next:

1. Save two copies of the spreadsheet you've made. Name one Written and the other Listening. Sort these so all of your listening and written skills come to the top of each spreadsheet.

Skill	Volume No.	Year Taught	Year Tested	Objective No.	Assessment Type					
					W	L	IP	S	F	DF
					W	L	IP	S	F	DF
					W	L	IP	S	F	DF
					W	L	IP	S	F	DF
					W	L	IP	S	F	DF
					W	L	IP	S	F	DF
					W	L	IP	S	F	DF
					W	L	IP	S	F	DF
					W	L	IP	S	F	DF
					W	L	IP	S	F	DF
					W	L	IP	S	F	DF
					W	L	IP	S	F	DF
					W	L	IP	S	F	DF
					W	L	IP	S	F	DF
					W	L	IP	S	F	DF
					W	L	IP	S	F	DF
					W	L	IP	S	F	DF
					W	L	IP	S	F	DF

W • Written   L • Listening   IP • Individual Performance   S • Summative (S)
F • Formative   DF • Department Final

FIGURE 28.

MUSICAL SKILLS TEMPLATE

2. Determine in which year you will test each skill. For example:
   a. Intervals (all major and perfect): Year 1
   b. Intervals (all major, perfect, minor): Year 2
   c. Intervals (all major, perfect, minor, diminished, and augmented): Years 3 and 4
3. Begin writing questions.

Listed below are seven guidelines for writing good questions and determining the number of questions per item. Test length does not have to be the same for different grades. Here is a suggested scenario:

Freshman Year:
- 100 multiple-choice theory questions
- 35 listening questions

Sophomore, Junior and Senior Years:
- 75 multiple-choice theory questions
- 42 listening questions

TIPS ON TEST WRITING

Test writing is an art in itself. While there is not space here to review guidelines for writing different kinds of tests, here are some general, overall tips for developing written tests.

1. *Create a table of specifications for your test.* List the content taught and the learning target.

   Suppose your learning target was for students to be able to name the four periods of music history. The key is the word "name." This means you want students to recall these periods from memory. This suggests that you should develop a short-answer rather than a multiple-choice question.

   Before making the test, review the content you have taught. It's great to have a written guide to help in test creation. Make sure that students have an opportunity to learn and an adequate amount of time to learn the content you chose before testing.

2. *Keep questions short and to the point.* Avoid long questions. A student may answer incorrectly because he didn't understand the question rather than because he doesn't know the content. Write questions using grade-level-appropriate language.

3. *Avoid double-barreled questions.* Make sure a question focuses on a single topic. Don't ask a question based on two ideas; students will be confused and not know how to answer.

4. *Make sure that there is only one correct answer.* In multiple-choice tests, this means that your response choices are mutually exclusive. In other words, they don't overlap. For True-or-False tests, take great care to avoid ambiguities. Some minds perceive ambiguities more easily than others. Strive for clear-cut questions.

5. *Provide clear directions on how to respond to the questions.*

6. *Make sure the number of questions you use for each content area corresponds to the amount of time you spent covering the content.*

    For example, if you spent one day on stringed instruments and three days on brass instruments, then your test should have more questions on brass instruments than on stringed instruments. It's not fair to include a large number of test items for areas on which you spent very little class time.

7. *Keep in mind that your test items should reflect your program goals.* As you develop written questions, remember to take the skills tested from the chart you created in Chapter 2.

There is a complete written test in Appendix D, and a listening test in Appendix E, both for a Year 1 student. There are also several complete tests and blank templates to help get you started on the accompanying disc. Before looking at some sample questions, please note that our written test questions are directly related to a published theory program. As a staff, we decided that students needed to have material available and usable. Students are given specific areas and volumes that are going to be taught and tested at the beginning of each year. Having a workbook and computer program, and reinforcing that material in the music taught each day, helps staff and students connect the theoretical to the practical (the music performed). Appendixes A–C present sample requirements for all four years. Here are Year 1 requirements, followed by some sample questions.

Volume	Unit	Items Tested
1	1	Staff, notes, pitches
1	2	Note values, time signatures, rests
1	3	Time signatures, ties, slurs
1	4	Repeats, eighth notes, dotted quarter notes
1	5	Dynamics, tempo marks, articulation, D. C., D. S.
1	6	Flats, sharps, naturals, whole and half steps, enharmonics
2	7	Tetrachords, scales, key signatures
2	8	Key signatures, chromatic scale, intervals
2	9	Intervals, solfège

FIGURE 29.

YEAR 1 TEST

SAMPLE WRITTEN QUESTIONS

1. Which clef is also known as the G clef?
   A) bass   B) alto   C) treble   D) tenor

2. Which clef is also known as a G clef?

Question 1 asks a first year student to select the correct clef with no visual cue. This is a knowledge-based question. Question 2 is the same question with visual cues.

How you ask the question depends on how you teach clef signs. Question 1 is one way to test clef understanding without software such as Sibelius for creating the music example in question 2. In question 1, students have to visualize the listed clef.

Question 2 is more appropriate if you want students to understand when playing that they may encounter clefs other than the one usually used for the music they perform and that they should recognize them by sight.

3. The note names of the five lines in the bass clef from bottom to top are:
   A) E–F–G–A–B   B) B–D–F–A–C   C) G–B–D–F–A   D) G–B–D–A–F

4. G–B–D–F–A are the names of the lines from bottom to top for which clef?

Questions 3 and 4 are two more examples of clef questions. Question 3 is designed for first year students and has no visual que. The question is narrow in focus and requires the student to think in only one clef. Question 4 asks for the same answer but uses other clefs as distractors.

Note that question design depends on how you are teaching the material. Note as well that no matter how you teach the material, understanding the lines and spaces in a clef is basic to music reading and understanding, and needs to be taught and tested.

5. Complete the given harmonic interval by choosing the name of the upper note.

   A: F♯   B: G♯   C: G   D: G♭

   Major 2nd

6. Name the interval shown.

    A: 3rd   B: 5th   C: 6th   D: 7th

7. Name the interval shown.

    A: P4   B: P5   C: M6   D: A5

8. Which example is a major third?

Questions 5–8 ask students to make or identify intervals. Question 5 asks for note names. Question 6 demonstrates a question designed for first-year students, since only the interval is tested, not its quality (major, minor, perfect, diminished, or augmented).

Question 7 is designed to keep the visual example simple, as question 6 does, but with interval quality added.

Question 8 brings the ideas behind questions 6 and 7 together by having four interval examples from which to choose.

9. Which example is a major third?

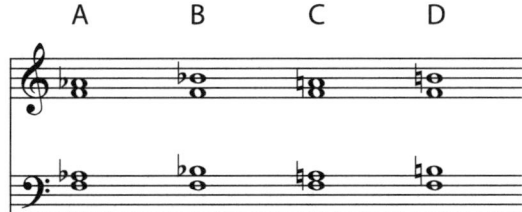

Question 9 features the grand staff, and allows students who read either treble or bass clef to answer the same question. If you believe that all students should understand both treble and bass clef, questions with grand staff examples in addition to single-clef questions allow you to test clefs with which the student is both more familiar and less familiar. The tests we have developed have questions with treble, bass, and grand staff questions. We feel it important for our students to be familiar with both treble and bass clefs. More advanced questions feature the grand staff exclusively, taking the variable of clef out of the question. It is more important on complex questions to let students find answers in the clef with which they are most familiar.

Our test results showed that first-year students could select intervals more accurately without music examples at first because accidentals were distracting. We suggest identifying intervals and triads in written tests for first-year students without accidentals early in the test, followed by questions with music examples containing accidentals later in the test.

These sample questions will help you get started writing questions and deciding how best to create music examples that help students understand the musical skills needed to become IMCQP. As noted above, there is a complete written test in Appendix D, and a listening test in Appendix E, both for a Year 1 student, as well as several complete tests and blank templates to help get you started on the accompanying disc.

ANALYSIS OF TEST DATA

One advantage of multiple-choice tests is that they can be electronically scored, saving time. Electronic scoring also makes possible test item analysis to determine student response patterns. An item analysis allows you to examine areas in which the students did well and areas where they performed poorly. We can use the data to help us make changes in teaching methods. Par Score is an example of an item analysis program.

In the next section we'll look at several examples of test data extracted from a written test. We'll see information about question reliability and more. The following definitions will help you understand the terminology used in the item analysis below. In Chapter 9, a more complete discussion will show you how to use item analysis data to improve both student and teacher performance.

INTERPRETING STANDARD ITEM ANALYSIS REPORTS

Item Analysis

The Standard Item Analysis Report is a statistical report that provides detailed distractor analysis based on raw scores. The reliability of a question, its difficulty, and/or effectiveness is statistically calculated. Low numbers of candidates taking the examination will produce statistics that will not be valid. Such statistics will only reveal whether your test was too easy or difficult for that particular group of applicants.

The Scantron Item Analysis includes:

- Total possible points
- Applicants in this group
- Standard deviation
- Median score
- Mean score
- Reliability coefficient (KR20)

- Highest score
- Lowest score
- An individual analysis for each applicant

The Standard Item Analysis Report expands the analysis and provides a point-biserial correlation coefficient (PBCC) as a discrimination value for each distractor. The PBCC is considered the single best measure of the effectiveness of a test item. Generally, the higher the PBCC, the better the discrimination, and thus the better the item. Typically, the following criteria may be used:

0.30 and above	Very good item
0.20 to 0.29	Reasonably good but subject to improvement
0.09 to 0.19	Marginal item, usually needs improvement
Below 0.09	Poor, to be rejected or improved

FIGURE 30.

POINT-BISERIAL INDICATION

A negative PBCC indicates that more candidates in the lower ability portion of the group responded correctly to the item than those in the higher ability portion of the group. PBCC is more affected by difficulty level, so a small applicant group will distort the number.

Item Analysis Report Explanation

Analysis available on the Standard Item Analysis Report:

Standard Deviation — a measure of variability computed by determining the square root of the variance

Applicants in Group — the number of Scantrons analyzed

Median Score — the point at or below which exactly 50% of the scores fall

Mean Score — the average score

Reliability Coefficient — the consistency of test items with each other which forms the total test score (a KR20 of 1.00 is perfect reliability)

Correct Group Response

Total — the percentage of the total group answering the item correctly

Upper 27% of Group — the percentage of the highest-scoring 27% of the candidates that answered that question correctly

Lower 27% of Group	the percentage of the lowest-scoring 27% of the candidates that answered that question correctly
Point Biserial Coefficient (PBCC)	the correlation between the correct answer on an item and the total test score of the candidate
Difficulty Index	how the candidate pool as a whole performed on a particular item (the closer the number is to 1.00, the greater the amount of candidates who got the question correct); an item that has a lower number (e.g., 0.20) indicates that the question was more difficult
Response Frequency	the number of responses to each possible answer A, B, C, D, and E if used
Non-distractors	An answer that zero percent of the group chose; items with low discrimination will, typically, have more than one non-distractor or the response frequencies will be especially low

HOW TO DEVELOP LISTENING ASSESSMENTS

Listening tests are created in the same way as written assessments. As suggested above for written tests, a review of the AP Music Theory tests at www.apmusictheory.com as well as the test-making capabilities of current music theory programs will help you in developing listening assessments.

In order to understand quality tests, seek out examples of tests and questions that help establish a standard. The written and listening areas of a test should be related. A broad-based set of skills that student musicians should develop will typically include a large percentage of listening skills, needed to perform music accurately and with a high level of musicality. Blending written and listening skills should be done over a series of years, allowing students to work on paper before advancing to the higher-level skill of listening.

Standard Item Analysis Report On Finl1 Version A

Course #:	06 Band Written yr1	Instructor:	Kimpton
Course Title:	Written Yr 1 Jan	Description:	2006 Yr 1 Written
Day/Time:		Term/Year:	

Total Possible Points:	91.00	Median Score:	70.17	Highest Score:	87.00
Standard Deviation:	10.75	Mean Score:	71.43	Lowest Score:	49.00
Student in this group:	30	Reliability Coefficient (KR20):	0.91		
Student Records Based On:	All Students				

No.	Correct Group Responses Total	Upper 27%	Lower 27%	Point Biserial	Correct Answer	A	B	C	D	E				Non Distractor
1	100.00%	100.00%	100.00%	0.00	A	*30	0	0	0	0				BCDE
2	93.33%	100.00%	87.50%	0.14	E	1	1	0	0	*28				CD
3	60.00%	62.50%	37.50%	0.20	C	2	8	*18	1	1				
4	56.67%	62.50%	25.00%	0.25	A	*17	1	2	9	1				
5	73.33%	100.00%	37.50%	0.53	C	0	1	*24	0	7				AD
6	76.67%	100.00%	37.50%	0.54	D	0	1	0	*23	6				AC
7	100.00%	100.00%	100.00%	0.00	D	0	0	0	*30	0				ABCE
8	80.00%	100.00%	75.00%	0.24	A	*24	2	3	1	0				E
9	83.33%	100.00%	50.00%	0.52	B	0	*25	0	3	2				AC
10	83.33%	100.00%	62.50%	0.45	D	0	0	4	*25	1				AB
11	93.33%	87.50%	100.00%	-0.24	D	2	0	0	*28	0				BCE
12	73.33%	100.00%	50.00%	0.32	E	2	0	5	1	*22				B
13	86.67%	100.00%	75.00%	0.31	A	*26	0	2	1	1				B
14	90.00%	100.00%	75.00%	0.34	A	*28	0	0	3	0				BCE
15	93.33%	100.00%	75.00%	0.35	B	0	*28	0	2	0				ACE
16	96.67%	100.00%	100.00%	0.04	E	0	0	0	1	*29				ABC
17	50.00%	87.50%	12.50%	0.56	C	0	4	*16	9	3				A
18	43.33%	87.50%	0.00%	0.63	D	15	0	1	*15	1				B
19	30.00%	50.00%	25.00%	0.27	D	16	1	2	*9	2				
20	73.33%	87.50%	50.00%	0.37	B	4	*22	2	2	0				E
21	66.67%	100.00%	37.50%	0.51	A	*21	7	2	1	1				
22	76.67%	100.00%	50.00%	0.47	E	1	1	5	0	*23				D
23	90.00%	100.00%	62.50%	0.63	D	0	0	1	*27	2				AB
24	56.67%	87.50%	37.50%	0.36	E	1	6	2	5	*17				
25	73.33%	87.50%	62.50%	0.34	B	3	*22	1	4	0				E
26	16.67%	0.00%	12.50%	-0.02	B	1	*5	3	1	20				
27	70.00%	100.00%	37.50%	0.53	C	3	0	*21	1	7				B
28	73.33%	100.00%	87.50%	0.13	E	3	1	1	3	*22				
29	86.67%	100.00%	87.50%	0.26	B	3	*27	1	0	0				DE
30	93.33%	100.00%	87.50%	0.12	A	*28	0	0	2	0				BCE
31	96.67%	100.00%	87.50%	0.15	E	1	0	0	0	*29				BCD
32	96.67%	100.00%	87.50%	0.15	A	*29	0	0	0	1				BCD
33	70.00%	100.00%	37.50%	0.59	E	3	2	0	4	*21				C
34	90.00%	100.00%	62.50%	0.53	D	0	1	1	*27	1				A
35	93.33%	100.00%	75.00%	0.41	A	*28	0	0	1	1				BC
36	76.67%	100.00%	75.00%	0.32	B	7	*26	0	0	0				CDE

Response Frequencies - * indicates correct answer

FIGURE 31.

STANDARD ITEM ANALYSIS REPORT ON FINL1 VERSION A

Students are given a printout of the questions missed. The test breakdown shows specific areas that need improvement. Chapter 9 discusses how students can use this print-out.

Student Test Report On Finl 1 A

Course #:   06 Band Written yr1   Instructor: Kimpton
Course Title: Written Yr 1 Jan   Description: 2006 Yr 1 Written
Day/Time: Term/Year:

Student Name:
Student ID: **Code:**

	Possible Pts.	Raw	Objective	Exam#/Essay	Percent	Grade
FINL 1:	91.00	84.00	84.00	0	92.31%	A

Response Description:

<dash>	correct response	<#>	multiple marks	<space>	no response
<alphabet>	student's incorrect response	<*>	bonus test item		

Test Items:	1-5	6-10	11-15	16-20	21-25	26-30	31-35	36-40	41-45	46-50
Answers	-,-,-,-,-	-,-,-,-,-	-,-,-,-,-	-,-,-,-,C	-,-,-,-,-	E,-,-,-,-	-,-,-,-,-	-,-,-,-,-	-,-,-,-,-	-,-,-,-,-

Test Items:	51-55	56-60	61-65	66-70	71-75	76-80	81-85	86-90	91-91
Answers	-,-,-,-,-	-,A,-,-,-	-,-,-,-,-	-,-,-,-,-	-,-,-,-,-	-,-,-,-,-	-,D,-,C,D	-,-,-,-,-	C

Remarks:

Student's Answer to Multiple Mark Question:

No multiple mark answers or answer keys found on this test.

FIGURE 32.

STUDENT TEST REPORT ON FINL1 VERSION A

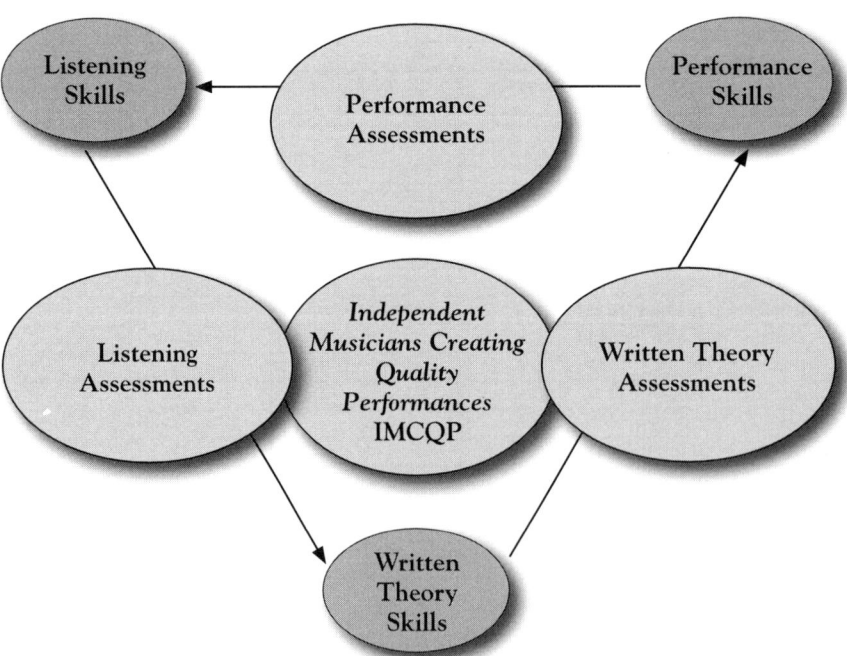

FIGURE 33.

Creating the listening portion of a test can be broken into a seven-part process.

1. Go back to your list of skills and objective sheet and note those you want to test in written and listening format.

2. Sort the spreadsheet named Listening you saved so all of the listening skills come to the top.

3. Determine in which year you will test each skill.

Skill	Volume No.	Year Taught	Year Tested	Objective No.	Assessment Type					
					W	L	IP	S	F	DF
					W	L	IP	S	F	DF
					W	L	IP	S	F	DF
					W	L	IP	S	F	DF
					W	L	IP	S	F	DF
					W	L	IP	S	F	DF
					W	L	IP	S	F	DF
					W	L	IP	S	F	DF
					W	L	IP	S	F	DF
					W	L	IP	S	F	DF
					W	L	IP	S	F	DF
					W	L	IP	S	F	DF
					W	L	IP	S	F	DF
					W	L	IP	S	F	DF
					W	L	IP	S	F	DF
					W	L	IP	S	F	DF
					W	L	IP	S	F	DF
					W	L	IP	S	F	DF

W • Written   L • Listening   IP • Individual Performance   S • Summative (Sum)
F • Formative   DF • Department Final

FIGURE 34.

MUSICAL SKILLS TEMPLATE

4. Begin writing questions. Sample listening questions to get you started follow.

A multiple-choice format that can be put on a Scantron sheet to be graded is the least time-consuming. This allows you to use data analysis software such as Par Score to study results.

5. Record test questions and write a script. Once you have written the listening questions, use a music processor such as Sibelius to play your examples.

6. Time the test to make sure it is not too long. Our listening test takes 35 minutes, which seems to be about the length of time our students can concentrate effectively. This 35-minute, 42-question listening test, combined with the 75-question written test, fit nicely into our school's 90-minute semester final exam time.

7. Lastly, sit down and record yourself announcing each question and playing the questions live at a piano. The AP Music Theory tests available at www.apmusictheory.com are excellent examples and a great beginning reference point.

SAMPLE LISTENING QUESTIONS

1. Which ascending interval is being played?

2. Which ascending interval is being played?

Question 1 gives students a visual music cue and asks them to select the correct ascending interval played. This helps young students to relate interval visual relationships with interval hearing-space relationships.

This is particularly important because this is what we want students to do when they play and read music. If students cannot see and hear an interval, how do they make corrections in the music they hear and play?

Question 2 is a higher-level hearing interval question for older students that offers no visual cue.

3. Which descending interval is being played?

4. Which descending interval is being played?

A: Major 2nd   B: Minor 3rd   C: Major 3rd   D: Perfect 4th

Questions 3 and 4 are interval questions designed for older students. The intervals are descending and are harder to hear and recognize. The questions are with and without visual cues for the reasons stated earlier. Recognizing ascending and descending intervals is a skill musicians need in order to hear, practice, and correct, in order to perform music accurately.

5. Which triad is being played?

6. Which triad is being played?

A: Major   B: Minor   C: Diminished   D: Augmented

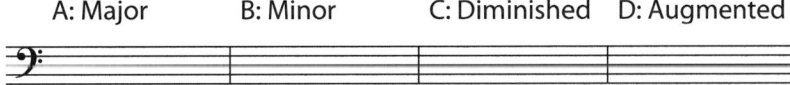

Questions 5 and 6 test the four triad forms with and without visual cues. Unlike the interval questions, our test results showed that students selected triads more accurately without visual cues at first, because accidentals in the music examples were distracting. We suggest identifying triads in the written test before putting music examples in the listening questions.

7. Which scale is being played?

8. Which scale is being played?

A: Major   B: Natural minor   C: Harmonic minor   D: Melodic minor

Questions 7 and 8 ask students to identify the four scale forms, with and without visual cues. In this case, accidentals were not distractors. In fact, the music examples helped students hear mistakes when practicing these scales and to write and understand how scales are constructed.

9. Which rhythm is being played?

Question 9 asks students to select the correct rhythm. Pitches are constant while rhythm varies. This is a skill which separates students who can count and visualize what patterns should sound like from those who have no idea how a rhythm should sound. In this example, bass and treble staves appear together instead of separately. Students should be able to recognize bass and treble notes on a written test. Combining the two for a listening test allows you to make one test for all.

10. Which example is being played?

Question 10 asks students to select which example is being played. In this example, the rhythms are constant but pitches are different. This skill is vital in order for musicians to hear, practice, correct, and perform music accurately.

These sample listening questions will help you get started writing questions and deciding how best to create music examples that help students hear the musical skills needed to become IMCQP. As noted above, there is a complete written test in Appendix D, and a listening test in Appendix E, both for a Year 1 student, as well as several complete tests and blank templates to help get you started on the accompanying disc.

SUMMARY

You have now completed another step as you *Scale Your Way to Music Assessment*. We hope you feel excited about this stage of professional growth. Your students should see new purpose in your teaching and you should feel a renewed motivation in rehearsal and the classroom. Your department can easily show on paper, through a variety of assessments, and more importantly, through individual performance, small group performance, and large group performance that your students are informed, independent musicians creating quality performances for others to enjoy.

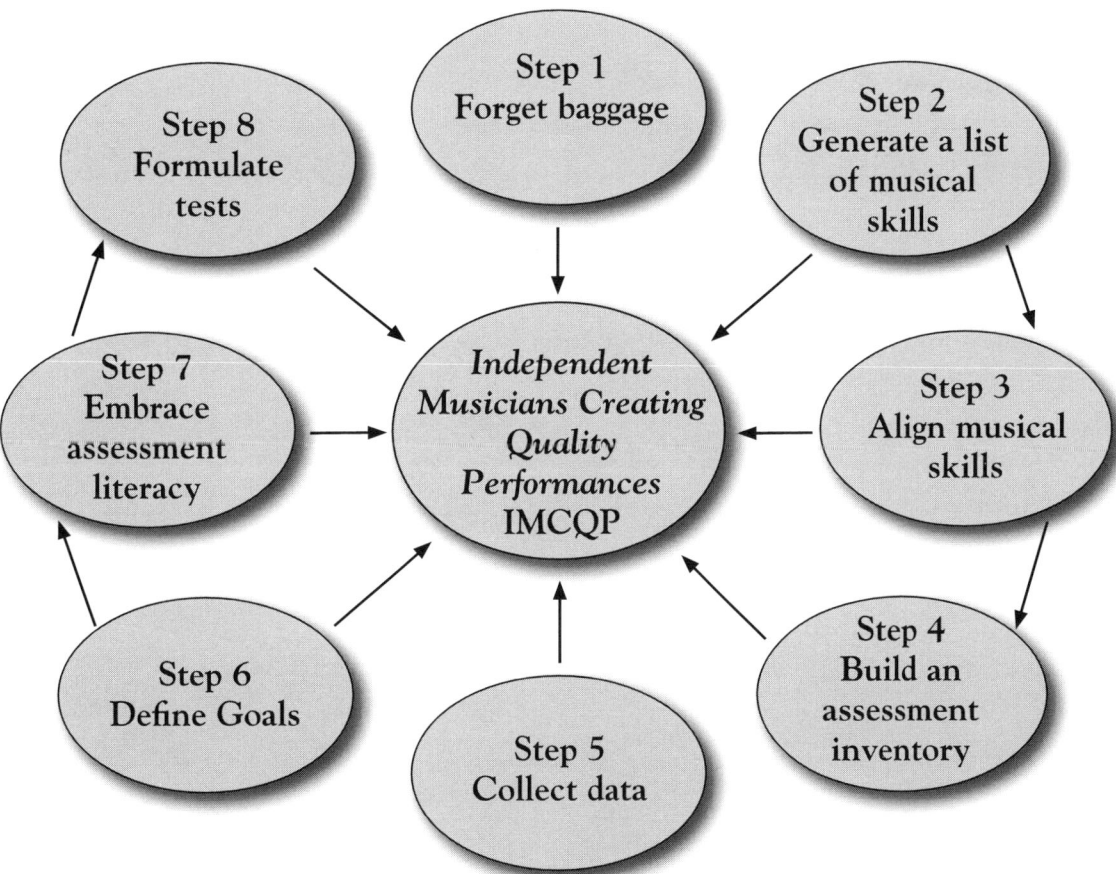

FIGURE 35.

CHAPTER 9

GEE! NOW YOU CAN EMPOWER LEARNERS AND EDUCATORS WITH ASSESSMENT RESULTS

If you have completed the eight steps to music assessment, you are ready to use the results to empower teachers, students, parents, and administrators to improve teaching and learning. Assessment data alone is of little value unless you use that data to improve your teaching and your students' understanding of their abilities. Teaching and learning are shared responsibilities. All stakeholders must work together to improve teaching and learning. It's very important for teachers not only to teach content and design quality assessments, but also to communicate their expectations and assessment results to students and parents.

Students will perform better if they know what is expected of them. Teachers need to clearly communicate their achievement targets to students and parents so that they will know what is expected. These targets also help parents know what educators expect of their students and provide them a way to become more involved in motivating their students at home to do their best. Administrators need to continue to support arts programs. Assessment data is key because it identifies areas in which students are excelling and areas in which additional support is needed.

This process begins with a clearly-defined plan for teaching. In addition to your lesson plans, it is important to have the following:

1. A list of skills to be taught and to what ages and grades. These skills form the foundation for building lesson plans.
2. A timeline of when testing will be done, including both formative and summative assessment.
3. A timeline for teacher planning, data entry, and data analysis.
4. Written, listening, and performance tests that truly measure what is taught.
5. Software to break the data down into understandable and usable information.
6. A delivery system for communicating to parents and students the requirements and the results of the assessments.

The next several pages will discuss:

1. Timelines for the year so that students and teachers will understand when testing and teaching should occur.
2. How to involve students in taking responsibility for improving skills.
3. How to use goal setting with students to improve performance.
4. How to develop assessments to improve instruction.

Let's begin with a sample plan for the year. The timeline below is for a high school, but the sequence can work for any grade level. The school year is broken into months, with one column for students, another for teachers. The Students column shows students' responsibilities and learning activities, while the Teachers column lists responsibilities for using data and providing educational leadership to students and parents.

AUGUST

Students	*Teachers*
	Receive test results from the preceding year's May jury performance, March solo contest, and item analysis of the June written and listening final.
	Results show weak and strong areas of individuals and classes.
	Begin planning music and class pacing.
	Discuss how to approach weak areas as a department (instead of leaving this to individual teachers).
	Question: How can you start teaching if you don't understand where students are in terms of written, listening, and performance skills?

SEPTEMBER

Students

Freshman and new students take a pre-test (approximately 30 minutes long) comprised of several questions on each skill that students are expected to learn during the year.

Are told the purpose for testing, how the assessment program works, and first-year expectations for playing, listening, and theory.

All students complete a skill-based performance (i.e., scales, tonal memory, etc.) as soon as possible in September.

Teachers

Receive results of pre-test and the voice testing of vocalists.

Instrumental staff hears each student perform a set of skills, including major and minor scales, chromatic scale, sightreading, and a prepared solo selection to get an understanding of each student's performance level.

Results show weak and strong areas of individuals and classes.

Begin planning music and class pacing. Discuss how to approach the weak areas as a department.

Question: How can you start teaching freshman or new students if you don't understand where they are in their written, listening, and performance skills?

OCTOBER

Students

Freshmen receive results from pre-test results.

Sophomores, Juniors, and Seniors receive results from the preceding year's May jury performance and March solo contest as well as an item analysis from the June written and listening final.

Write the average of each performance area on the rubric score sheet.

Make written comments on scores received and how they will improve each area.

Set a target score for each area for the end-of-year May Jury.

Mark incorrect answers on written and listening test questions for current volume of theory book to note areas for improvement and strong skill areas.

Teachers

Hand out test results and letter to students and parents explaining results.

Review student test forms and yearly performance, written, and listening goals.

NOVEMBER

Students	Teachers
Attend honors recital with a copy of soloists' music to study during performance.	Review national music rubric and vocabulary list with students before honors recital.
Use national rubric to rate honors students' performance; write comments using vocabulary from vocabulary skill list.	Meet with honors students individually after honors recital to review performance video.
Honors students watch video of themselves with teacher and rate themselves using the national form; receive copy of students' comments and teacher rating.	Compare teacher and student self-evaluation with student; discuss any differences.
	Teach grade-appropriate skills through in-class music or from theory book or computer program.
Write a 1,000-word paper on a composition and its composer.	
Learn grade-appropriate skills through in-class music.	
Use theory book or computer program to improve weak skills.	

DECEMBER/MID-JANUARY

Students	Teachers
Continue learning skills to prepare for semester final.	Teach skills through in-class music; test student understanding.

MID-JANUARY

Students	Teachers
Take written and listening semester final (summative) on required skills.	Give written and listening semester final (summative) on required skills.
	Note: We believe in front-loading, or teaching all skills for the year in the first semester, then applying and mastering those skills during the second semester.

LATE JANUARY

Students	Teachers
Receive item analysis from first semester final.	
Mark incorrect answers on first semester final questions for current volume of theory book to note areas for improvement and strong skill areas.	

LATE JANUARY/EARLY MARCH

Students	Teachers
Begin working on individual solos for contest.	Lead students to take more responsibility for skill progress, allowing more instruction on music.
Participate in an ensemble for contest.	
Are expected to apply all skills learned in solo and ensemble music preparation.	Stress phrasing, interpretation, and overall musicianship.
	Teachers work with students encouraging them to be independent learners whenever possible.

MID-MARCH

Students	Teachers
Receive results from the March solo contest.	Review jury requirements and guide students in selecting music to be performed.
Write the average of each performance area on the rubric score sheet.	
Make written comments on scores received and how they will improve each area.	
Set a target score for each area for the end-of-year May jury.	

LATE MARCH

Students	Teachers
Begin working on May jury selections, applying performance skills without help from staff or private teachers.	Discuss appropriateness of May jury selections with students.
Note: This gives the chance to demonstrate ability to apply skills learned.	

APRIL

Students	Teachers
Continue working on jury selections and mastering skills (not learning new ones in rehearsal).	Reinforce performance and theory skills in rehearsal (no new skills are taught).
Reinforce theory skills for June final through rehearsal.	Emphasize mastery of the skills taught in the first semester.

MAY

Students	Teachers
Give final performances.	
Play a solo, required scales, triads, and sightreading for a panel of judges.	

JUNE

Students	Teachers
Take second semester written and listening skills final.	Give second semester written and listening skills final.
	Enter data from second semester final and May juries into assessment software.

FIGURE 36.

TIMELINE FOR ONE YEAR

SUMMARY OF TIMELINE

Breaking down the school year into months and activities reveals that the actual time spent with students is very short. Because of this, it's important to maximize teaching time to ensure that students are given specific targeted information and skills at appropriate times. Wasting student contact time with unplanned rehearsals or classes does not create independent musicians; it creates dependent musicians who are not being challenged, musically or intellectually. We need to use performance music to reinforce the skills taught so students can make the connection between what is being taught and the music they are performing. Motivating students to learn new theory and listening skills is easy if they see that those skills create a greater understanding of the music and that they are thus performing at a higher level. Students will see the connection between music content skills and music performed. If the teacher does not help students make this connection, students will see skills as something they need to learn for a test and then forget.

HOW TO INVOLVE STUDENTS IN TAKING RESPONSIBILITY FOR IMPROVING SKILLS

We developed a music planning sheet years ago because it seemed we were always asking the same questions or teaching the same material. How often have you had to stop rehearsal and ask the students what a term means because they were not demonstrating the musical term through their performance? A dollar for each question about dynamics, such as, "What does *mf* mean?" would make you a millionaire. After using music planning sheets, students began to take increasing responsibility to understand skills and terms and to demonstrate their understanding through performances. We found that by using music planning sheets, students were highly motivated to learn those skills and made connections to other music they were performing. Figure 37 presents an example of a solo worksheet. Note that the student must complete the sheet, thus encouraging independent application of musical skills.

The solo worksheet should be completed after the teacher completes a model worksheet based on a selection students are actually playing. Students need to understand the teacher's expectations of quality, what each area means musically, and what skills they need to perform. Going over the teacher's model worksheet with students helps them accomplish this.

Once students have studied the model worksheet, they should complete a solo worksheet on their own for each selection they are performing. The worksheet is then graded and returned to students for immediate feedback. Students learn to assess the music they are playing and what skills are needed in each area in order to perform accurately and musically. The teacher sees the students' insight (or lack of it) into their musical understanding, and can provide feedback. This process is designed to promote Independent Musicians Creating Quality Performances (IMCQP).

Name_____

Title_____ Composer_____ Genre _____

In order to perform your solo correctly, it is important to understand everything that is written and notated by the composer. You will be asked to write the definitions of all the terms written on your music in addition to writing out how to count the rhythms in your solo. Answer the following questions and return it in your binder at the end of band on Friday. Since this is being done in class, I will expect a very detailed and neat assignment.

Keys in your solo: Name your scale (not concert pitch) and write it on the staff paper attached.

1_____ 2_____ 3_____ 4_____

Write the intervals you need to be able to play on the staff paper attached.

m2   M2   m3   M3   P4   P5   m6   M6   m7   M7   P8
more than an octave

Tempo marking   Definition   Metronome   Meter
1_____   _____   _____   _____

2_____   _____   _____   _____

3_____   _____   _____   _____

Musical Terms/Symbols   Definition
1_____   _____

2_____   _____

3_____   _____

4_____   _____

5_____   _____

Time signatures: List them below and what top and bottom numbers mean.

_____   _____   _____

Rhythms: Notate each one once and write out the counts under the rhythm.

_____   _____   _____

_____   _____   _____

_____   _____   _____

Figure 37.
Solo Worksheet

Self-assessment is another way to lead students to take responsibility for improving skills. The next few pages detail the delivery system we use for encouraging students to self-assess and set goals for improvement that create Independent Musicians Creating Quality Performances. There are letters to parents, students, test results from performances, listening and written test results, and test questions broken down into volumes and categories.

Students are asked to reflect on test results to determine areas of strength and weakness. Students must interpret test results on their own if they are to develop deep musical understanding. Taking ownership of test results encourages students to see assessment in a positive way as they identify their strengths. This process also motivates students to set goals that will remediate their areas of weakness. This helps students move from short term to long term; in other words, they begin thinking about daily, weekly, and monthly skill development.

For example, can you imagine sitting down with students, discussing how to improve tone or intonation? What a collaborative, educational experience that would be for the teacher and student! Goal setting is a vital part of a child's education. Learning to set and complete goals can be a secret to student success in music and in life. Goal setting is discussed in Chapter 10.

To all students:

Attached is your jury performance, written final, and listening final answer sheet from your May music department final or freshman pre-test. We are asking you to:

Jury Performance: RETURN IN BINDER

1. Mark on the national form your final score in the circles to the left of the sheet.

2. In each box on the right, write how you will improve your score and what musical exercises you will do to improve your score.

Written final and listening final: RETURN IN BINDER

1. Circle on the attached sheet any questions you missed. Each page has a heading that specifies listening or written.

    a. Dash = correct answer

    b. Letter = incorrect answer you gave

2. Find time to go to the computer lab in the band room and work on the weak areas you have found. The lab hours are Monday through Thursday 7:30–8:00 a.m. and 3:00–3:30 p.m.

    a. If you would like to purchase the workbook we are using, you may do so in the band office.

3. Extra credit will be given for tests taken on the software with a score of 90 or above.

By doing this you will see the areas you are weak or strong in and can then begin to work on improving any weak areas. This will be a combined effort by the student and the teacher to improve the musical areas that are weak and develop the skills that are new this year. You will notice that the questions are broken down into types, units, and volume numbers, so you will be able to find them and use the music software in the piano lab to help understand weak areas. If you would like to purchase the theory workbook, you may do so in the band office.

Remember that another form of this test will be taken in January and June for the semester finals. We hope you take the time to improve your understanding of music. Each year has a different set of performance, written theory, and listening examples and builds on the skills developed over the previous year.

Please ask your parents to sign that you have seen the test and completed the answer guide and are aware of what areas you need to improve.

The staff is making a major push to insure that all students understand the musical skills needed to become a self-directed musician.

Please return the attached sheet signed and completed to your director by Thursday, October 20th IN YOUR BINDER.

I have attached below the criteria the student's performances were rated on numerically.

5	A superior performance	outstanding in nearly every detail
4	An excellent performance	minor defects

3   A good performance   lacking finesse and/or interpretation

2   A fair performance   basic weaknesses

1   A poor performance   unsatisfactory

The areas that are assessed are:

Tone Quality   resonance, control, clarity, focus, consistency, warmth

Intonation   accuracy to printed pitches

Rhythm   accuracy of notes and rest values, duration, pulse, steadiness, correctness of meters

Technique (facility/accuracy) artistry, attacks, releases, control of ranges, musical and/or mechanical skills

Interpretation, Musicianship style, phrasing, tempo, dynamics, emotional involvement

Diction   vocal

Bowing   strings

Articulation   winds

Other Performance Factors   choice of literature, appropriate appearance, poise, posture, general conduct, mannerisms, facial expression (vocal), memory

Scales, intervals, triads

Student Signature _____   Date_____

Parent Signature _____   Date_____

FIGURE 38.

STUDENT LETTER FOR TEST AND PERFORMANCE ASSESSMENT

Category	CONTEST	Judge 1	Judge 2	Judge 3	Judge 4	Judge 5	Total
Student Name							
Tone Quality	4	3.5	3.5	4	4	4	3.83
Intonation	5	4	4	4	5	3	4.16
Rhythm	5	4	4	4.5	3.5	5	4.33
Technique	5	4	4	4	4.5	4	4.25
Interpretation/ musicianship	5	3	3	3.5	4.5	3	3.66
Diction/bowing/ articulation	5	4	4	4	4	4	4.16
Performance factors	5	4	4	5	5	5	4.66
Scales/Triads	5	4	4	5	4	5	4.5

5	A superior performance	outstanding in nearly every detail
4	An excellent performance	minor defects
3	A good performance	lacking finesse and/or interpretation
2	A fair performance	basic weaknesses
1	A poor performance	unsatisfactory

Areas assessed are:

Tone Quality	resonance, control, clarity, focus, consistency, warmth
Intonation	accuracy to printed pitches
Rhythm	accuracy of notes and rest values, duration, pulse, steadiness, correctness of meters
Technique (facility/accuracy)	artistry, attacks, releases, control of ranges, musical and/ or mechanical skills
Interpretation, Musicianship	style, phrasing, tempo, dynamics, emotional involvement
Diction	vocal
Bowing	strings
Articulation	winds
Other Performance Factors	choice of literature, appropriate appearance, poise, posture, general conduct, mannerisms, facial expression (vocal), memory
Scales, intervals, triads	

On the attached National Adjudication Form

1. Write your scores in the boxes next to the categories that match your scores.

2. Write in the box to the right of your score a target score for this year.

3. Next to the target score for the year, write what you will need to do to improve. If you are unsure of how to improve your score, make an appointment to see your teacher.

FIGURE 39.

INDIVIDUAL PERFORMANCE RESULTS FROM CONTEST AND JURY

NFHS MUSIC ADJUDICATION FORM
SOLO

Order of Appearance: <u>Click & Add</u>   Date: <u>Click & Add</u>   Program/Event No.: <u>Click & Add</u>

Event: <u>Click & Add</u>   Class: <u>Click & Add</u>
(tenor solo, trumpet solo, etc.)

School Name: <u>Click & Add</u>   Location-Contest/Festival: <u>Click & Add</u>

Name of Soloist: <u>Click & Add</u>

Selections	Composer	Publisher
1._____	_____	_____
2._____	_____	_____
3._____	_____	_____

Place one of these numbers in each box below, then total carefully.

5 — A superior performance — outstanding in nearly every detail.   2 — A fair performance — basic weaknesses.
4 — An excellent performance — minor defects.   1 — A poor performance — unsatisfactory.
3 — A good performance — lacking finesse and/or interpretation.

	AREAS OF CONCERN	COMMENTS
	Tone Quality Consider: resonance, control, clarity, focus, consistency, warmth	
	Intonation Consider: accuracy to printed pitches	
	Rhythm Consider: accuracy of note and rest values, duration, pulse, steadiness, correctness of meters	
	Technique (facility/accuracy) Consider: artistry, attacks, releases, control of ranges, musical and/or mechanical skill	
	Interpretation, Musicianship Consider: style, phrasing, tempo, dynamics, emotional involvement	
	Diction - Vocal **Bowing - Strings** **Articulation - Winds**	
	Other Performance Factors Consider: Choice of literature, appropriate appearance, poise, posture, general conduct, mannerisms, facial expression (vocal), memory (if required)	
	Sight-Reading, Scales	

TOTAL POINTS

_____
(signature of adjudicator)

Divisional Rating _____

RATING COMPUTATION TABLE

Without Sight-Reading		With Sight-Reading
35-32 points =	Division I (Superior)	= 40-36 points
31-25 points =	Division II Excellent)	= 35-28 points
24-18 points =	Division III (Good)	= 27-20 points
17-11 points =	Division IV (Fair)	= 19-12 points
10-7 points =	Division V (Poor)	= 11-8 points

NFHS
PO Box 690
Indianapolis, IN 46206
Phone: 317-972-6900; Fax:317.822.5700
www.nfhs.org

FIGURE 40.

NFHS MUSIC ADJUDICATION FORM (SOLO)

Student Test Report On Exam 1 A

Course #:   07 Band Written Yr 1   Instructor: Kimpton07
Course Title: Band Written 07 yr 1   Description: 2007 Yr1 Written
Day/Time: Term/Year:

Student Name:

Student ID: **Code:**

	Possible Pts.	Raw	Objective	Exam#/Essay	Percent	Grade
EXAM 1:	91.00	84.00	84.00	0	92.31%	A

Response Description:

<dash>	correct response	<#>	multiple marks	<space>	no response
<alphabet>	student's incorrect response	<*>	bonus test item		

Test Items:	1-5	6-10	11-15	16-20	21-25	26-30	31-35	36-40	41-45	46-50
Answers	-,-,-,-,-	-,-,-,-,E	-,-,-,-,-	-,-,-,-,-	-,-,-,-,-	-,-,-,-,-	-,-,-,-,-	-,-,-,-,-	-,-,-,-,-	-,-,-,-,-

Test Items:	51-55	56-60	61-65	66-70	71-75	76-80	81-85	86-90	91-91	
Answers	-,A,-,-,-	-,-,-,-,-	-,-,-,-,-	B,-,A,A,-	-,-,-,-,-	-,-,-,-,-	-,-,-,C,A	-,-,-,-,-	-	

Remarks:

Student's Answer to Multiple Mark Question:

No multiple mark answers or answer keys found on this test.

FIGURE 41.

STUDENT TEST REPORT ON FINL 1A

Interval Recognition: Visual	Questions 1–5
Correct Notation: Listening	Questions 6–10
Rhythm and Notes	Questions 11–15
Rhythm	Questions 16–20
Intervals: Not Visual	Questions 21–32
Triads: Not Visual	Questions 33–37
Intervals: Visual	Questions 38–42

FIGURE 42.

YEAR 2 LISTENING FINAL BREAKDOWN

Volume	Unit	Description	Questions
1	1	Staff, notes and pitches	1–13
1	6	Flats, sharps, naturals, whole and half steps, enharmonics	14–25
2	8	Key signatures, chromatic scale, intervals	26–41
2	9	Intervals continued, solfège	42–55
Terms, goal setting			56–75

FIGURE 43.

YEAR 2 WRITTEN TEST BLUEPRINT

After taking time to read and consider this way of involving students in taking responsibility for skill improvement, answer this question:

How can I take this information and
apply it to my situation to help create Independent
Musicians Creating Quality Performances?

_____
_____
_____
_____
_____
_____
_____
_____
_____
_____
_____
_____
_____
_____
_____
_____

A DELIVERY SYSTEM IN A BINDER:
A STORY FROM PAUL KIMPTON

I developed the Binder system fourteen years ago in a moment of desperation. I had to come up with a way to have students prepare music and other long-term assignments without procrastination. The revelation came to me when I found myself coming home and saying, "Well, I hope we get through this concert," or whining before the final rehearsals for a concert, "I don't understand why you can't play these measures," or "I can't believe we are a week away from a performance, and you aren't playing the dynamics."

After one of those rehearsals, I asked a student how he felt about my comments. His answer is embedded in my mind. First, the student hesitated, wondering if he should answer the question honestly. Once the student came to the conclusion that I wanted a genuine response, he said, "We don't mind your comments about our level of performance, but what we do mind is that you are saying it to everyone when we know it only applies to a few students. When you make those comments to the entire band, we all take it personally. We want you to tell the students who are not meeting expectations what they need to do." Wow—he was right. I thought about how I would react if general negative comments were made to me which I knew did not apply to me. I would be frustrated. Hence, I created the Binder system, which is a way for students to take responsibility for making rehearsals and their practice productive, and music skill development the focus of their efforts.

A music binder is a weekly breakdown of each quarter for the year. Each week is broken down into:

1. Days of the week
2. Date of the week
3. Various categories, such as band music, lesson music, solo music, theory, etc.
4. Beginning and ending practice times
5. Specific measures and focus of practice

Ask students to plan one week at a time, and then reflect on that plan on a review sheet at the end of the week as they create the next week's plan sheet. Ask students to turn the assignment in on a table in the front of the band room, or another convenient spot. Read and make suggestions or give encouragement. The plan sheet asks students when they are going to practice and on what specific areas in the music they will focus. This means that students have to assess the difficulty of the music and develop a timeline to prepare the music at least two weeks before a concert. Have students play for you two weeks before the concert. This encourages individual accountability. Students cannot hide in a section when they have to play by themselves.

Rehearsals before a concert will take on a whole new tone when the focus is on the nuances of the music. The binder, plan sheets, and review sheets have become a tradition for us, developing an effective dialogue between student and teacher. As many schools focus on improving student writing skills, the music department can take an active role, all the while training students in planning for success. The binder becomes the delivery system for the assessment program, as it contains all the materials necessary to create an environment for student success: performance dates, syllabus, worksheets, percussion music, solos, homework, plan and review sheets, grading policy, and points for each quarter. Students can develop a plan for the each day and week so they can reach their long-term goals.

Here are examples of a third-quarter teacher and student goals sheet, a weekly plan sheet, and a weekly review sheet. These will give you a better idea about how we use the binder to help students reach their potential.

Due _____

Our short- and long-term goals are listed below. Please list some short- and long-term goals you would like to work on. Remember that when you write your goal, you are making a commitment to following through. Remember to make reasonable goals that you can achieve.

1. Short-term goal: All ensemble members and music selected January 30th. All ensemble/solo events sent to IHSA January 31st.

2. Short-term goal: Have all solos assigned to accompanist February 10th.

3. Short-term goal: Music selected for spring concert, March 10th.

4. Long-term goal: Have all band music learned by April 13th.

What are several short- or long-term goals you would like to work on this quarter? Be as specific as you can.

General
_____

_____

Music skill
_____

_____

Music skill
_____

_____

Theory Goal
_____

_____

Listening Goal
_____

_____

FIGURE 44.

GOALS SHEET

This is our third quarter of plan sheets. I will not accept sloppy and vague forms, since you have two major selections to have ready for performance. I must see specific comments on what you are practicing and also your name and correct dates. Each sheet is worth 6 pts.

Name_____Due / / Student #_____

Luck
There is no such thing as luck; only the ability to
Labor Under Correct Knowledge

Friday   Date _____   Start Time _____   End Time _____
Band / Perc. / Ensemble / Solo / Lesson / Scale   Section/Measures   What is the focus?

                                                                  _____   _____

Saturday   Date _____   Start Time _____   End Time _____
Band / Perc. / Ensemble / Solo / Lesson / Scale   Section/Measures   What is the focus?

                                                                  _____   _____

Sunday   Date _____   Start Time _____   End Time _____
Band / Perc. / Ensemble / Solo / Lesson / Scale   Section/Measures   What is the focus?

                                                                  _____   _____

Monday   Date _____   Start Time _____   End Time _____
Band / Perc. / Ensemble / Solo / Lesson / Scale   Section/Measures   What is the focus?

                                                                  _____   _____

Tuesday   Date _____   Start Time _____   End Time _____
Band / Perc. / Ensemble / Solo / Lesson / Scale   Section/Measures   What is the focus?

                                                                  _____   _____

Wednesday   Date _____   Start Time _____   End Time _____
Band / Perc. / Ensemble / Solo / Lesson / Scale   Section/Measures   What is the focus?

                                                                  _____   _____

Thursday   Date _____   Start Time _____   End Time _____
Band / Perc. / Ensemble / Solo / Lesson / Scale   Section/Measures   What is the focus?

                                                                  _____   _____

FIGURE 45.

PLANNING SHEET

Review sheet for week _____

Name_____Due / / Student #_____

2 Days until you play your solo with piano!!!!!!!!

0 Days until your ensemble starts playing for the band—Graded.

9 Days until Contest.

Did you turn in your P. E. Exemption as requested? Remember, you were asked to return it even if you are not taking the exemption and write on the form "I am not taking the exemption."

How many times did you practice your solo? _____

How many times outside of band did your ensemble practice?_____Remember you are to meet once a week (5pts.).

You were asked to be able to count your solo aloud in tempo. Can you do it?

   Yes or No   If you say Yes and can not do it in band or for me, then this review will be a zero!

Can you play your chromatic or rudiments without mistakes up and down?

   Yes or No   If you say Yes and can not do it in band or for me, then this review will be a zero!

Can you play your scales or rudiments up and down without mistakes!

   Yes or No   If you say Yes and can not do it in band or for me, then this review will be a zero!

You will play with your piano player next week. Can you play straight through your solo after having it for the last eight weeks?

   Yes or No   If you say yes and can not do it in band or for me, then this review will be a zero!

What three tuning notes will you use?

   1 _____ 2 _____ 3 _____   Remember to use notes from your solo that you hold out or are played numerous times. Always do one as concert B-flat.

What did you get done on your solo? _____

What did you get done on your ensemble?_____

What will you do differently this week? _____

FIGURE 46.

REVIEW SHEET

Now that you have had some time to consider this way of involving students in goal setting, answer the following question:

How can I take this information and
apply it to my situation to help create Independent
Musicians Creating Quality Performances?

_____
_____
_____
_____
_____
_____
_____
_____
_____
_____
_____
_____
_____
_____

We have seen three examples of how students can improve performances through assessment. Now it is time to see how teachers can use assessment to improve instruction. Having assessment information but not using it to improve instruction would be the greatest loss of all. The community of teachers as learners needs to strive continuously to improve the art and science of teaching. What better way to improve teaching than by looking at what students understand and don't understand? With that information, we can look at how we use performance data to focus rehearsals on improving weak performance factors.

Below are several graphs of data on performance factors. Figure 47 shows data for each senior jury for a four-year period. When our teachers first saw the jury performance data from 2000 as visual and numerical graphs, a major change took place. That graph brutally displayed student performance factors as seen by professional musicians. It was not teachers making inflated judgments of their students' abilities; instead it was an objective assessment of the musical abilities of our students—one that they would face if they performed in the real world. The data showed teachers areas for potential improvement of instruction. Before we could take action, however, we had to answer several difficult questions.

1. What were we doing that was not getting the results we thought we were getting?
2. Were we going to believe the data and open ourselves up to change?
3. What changes could we make in our teaching?
4. Did we owe it to our students to openly address the areas we felt were weak?
5. Could we work collaboratively as a department to change the weak areas?

Can you imagine the discussions we had? The staff had a lot to deal with in order to consciously make some changes. If you look at the data, you can see that we faced the facts, got down to work, and targeted several key areas. The data speaks to improvement over time when the scores from each year are compared to the next. This data is broken down into separate performance areas. The five years of data show significant growth in almost every area. The staff now looks forward to analyzing the data each year in order to understand what is working or not working in our classrooms.

Take some time to study the data, and answer the following questions.

1. How would you change your teaching to address the issues you see in the data?
2. What do you think the data tells you about your students?
3. How would you involve your students in improving weak areas?

PART ONE: DATA FROM SENIOR STUDENTS YEARS 1–5

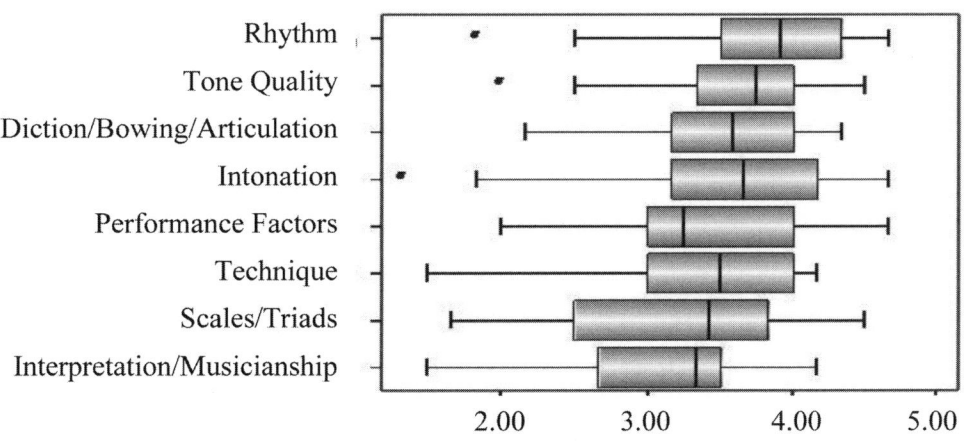

FIGURE 47.

YEAR 1: ALL EIGHT CRITERIA

MAY YEAR 1

SENIOR JURY AND MARCH SOLO CONTEST DATA

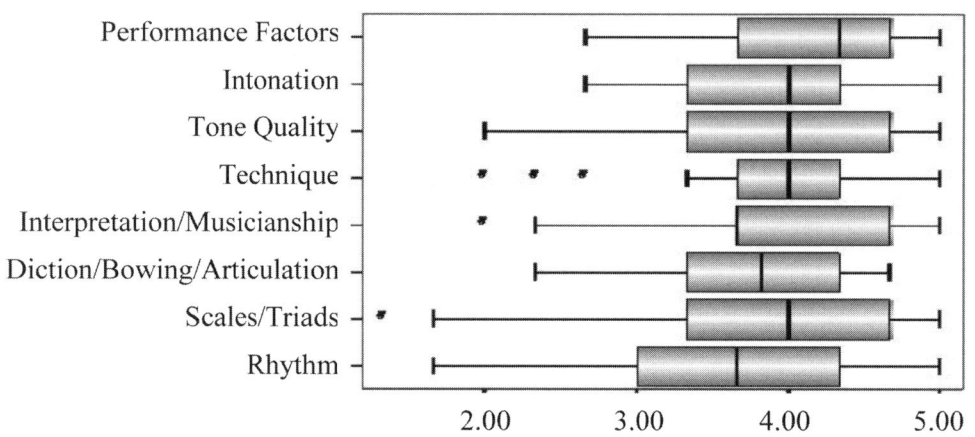

FIGURE 48.

YEAR 2: ALL EIGHT CRITERIA

MAY YEAR 2

SENIOR JURY AND MARCH SOLO CONTEST DATA

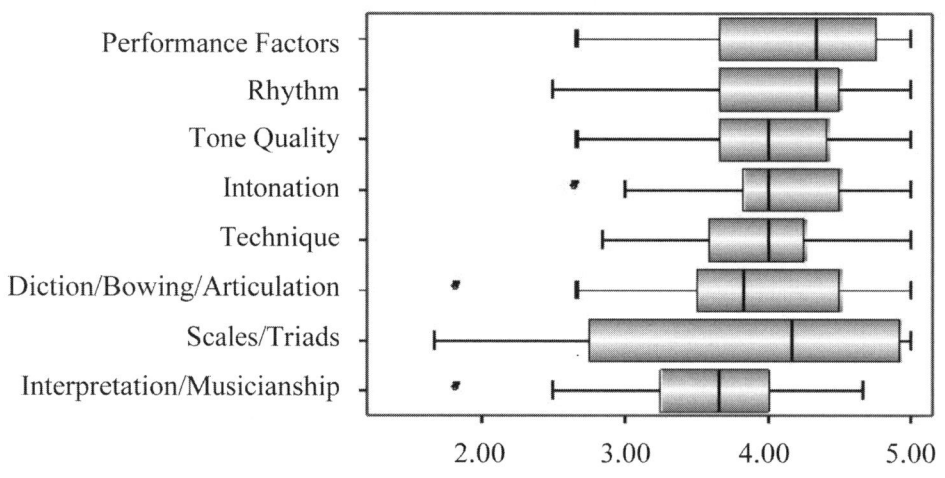

FIGURE 49.

YEAR 3: ALL EIGHT CRITERIA

MAY YEAR 3

SENIOR JURY AND MARCH SOLO CONTEST DATA

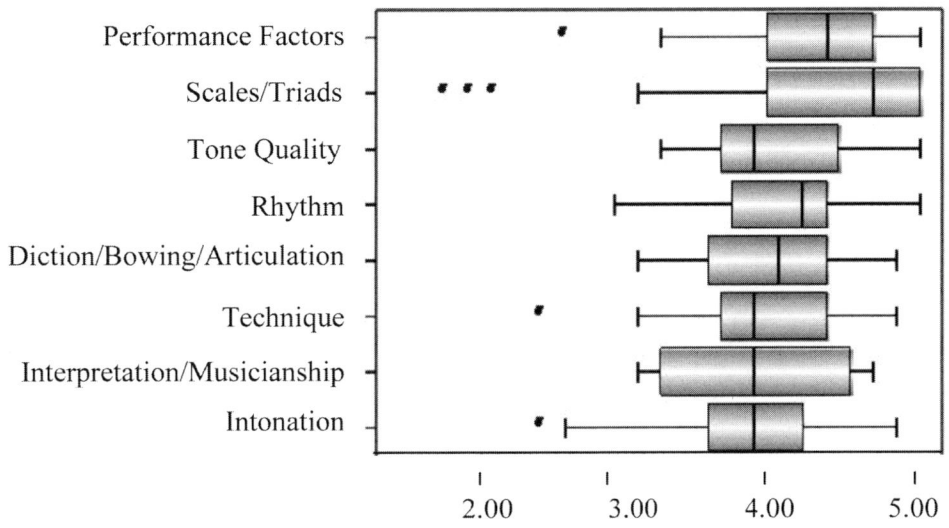

FIGURE 50.
YEAR 4: ALL EIGHT CRITERIA
MAY YEAR 4
SENIOR JURY AND MARCH SOLO CONTEST DATA

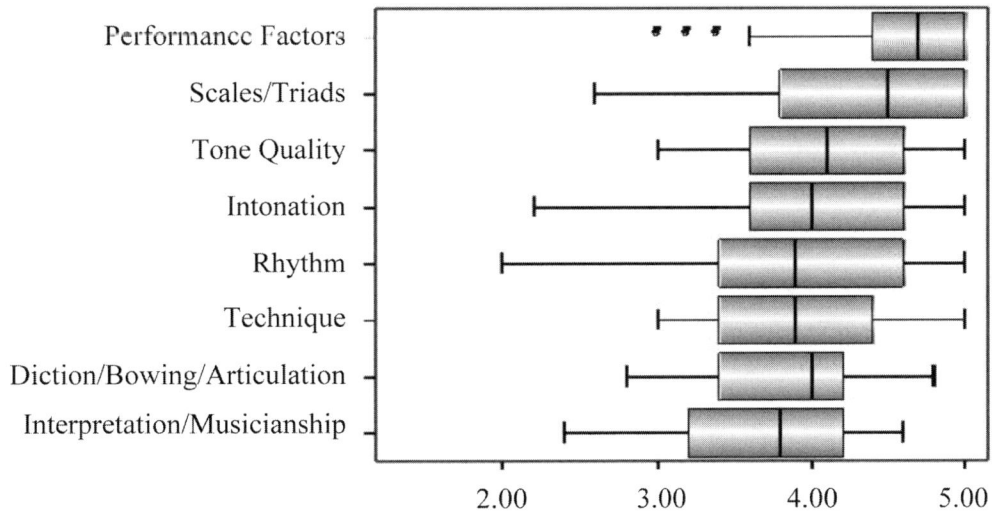

FIGURE 51.
YEAR 5: ALL EIGHT CRITERIA
MAY YEAR 5
SENIOR JURY AND MARCH SOLO CONTEST DATA

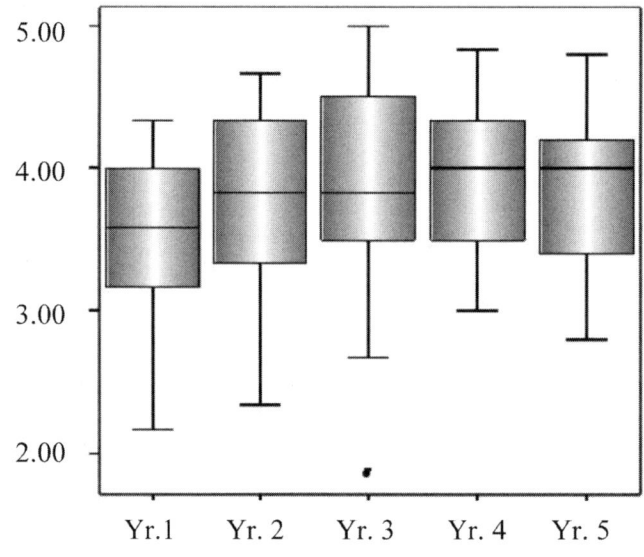

FIGURE 52.

ALL FIVE YEARS

SENIOR STUDENT PERFORMANCE DATA ACROSS FIVE YEARS

CRITERION 1: DICTION, BOWING, AND ARTICULATION

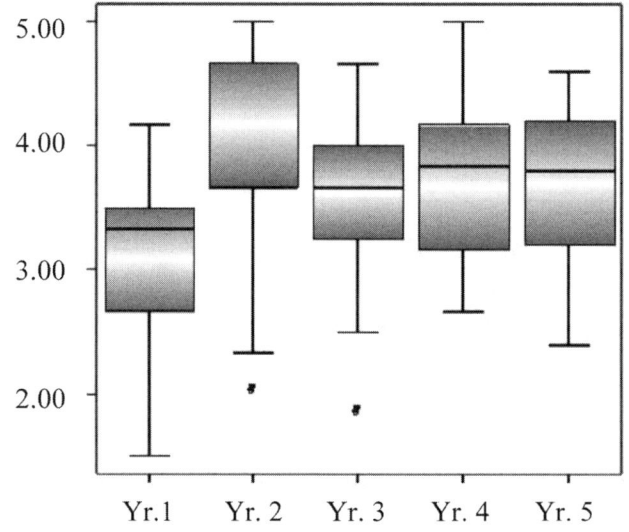

FIGURE 53.

ALL FIVE YEARS

SENIOR STUDENT PERFORMANCE DATA ACROSS FIVE YEARS

CRITERION 2: INTERPRETATION AND MUSICIANSHIP

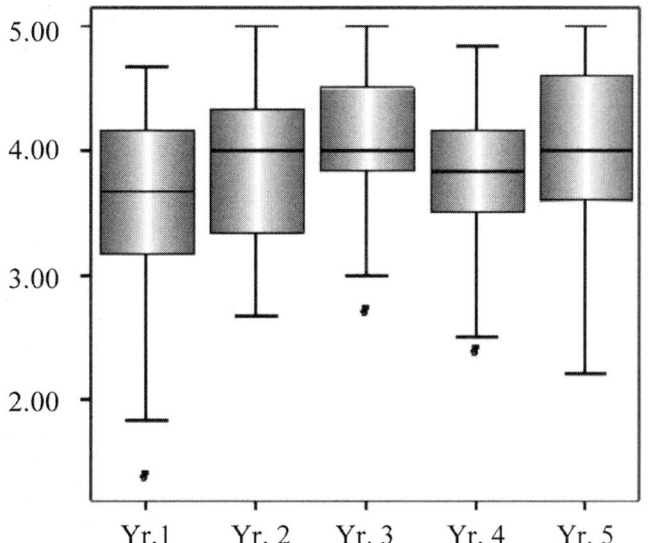

FIGURE 54.

ALL FIVE YEARS

SENIOR STUDENT PERFORMANCE DATA ACROSS FIVE YEARS

CRITERION 3: INTONATION

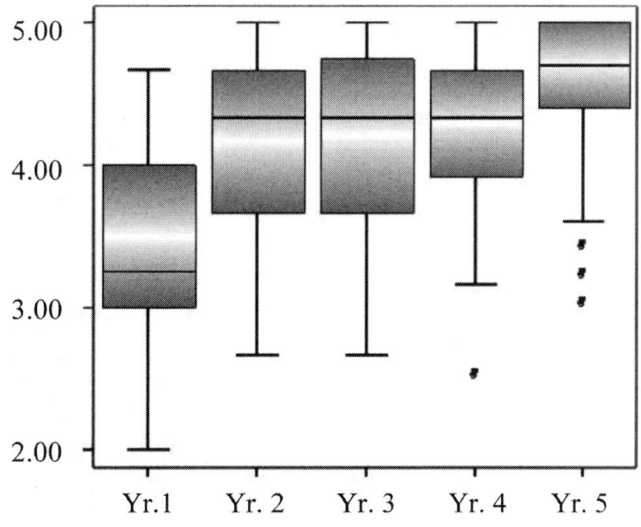

FIGURE 55.

ALL FIVE YEARS

SENIOR STUDENT PERFORMANCE DATA ACROSS FIVE YEARS

CRITERION 4: PERFORMANCE FACTORS

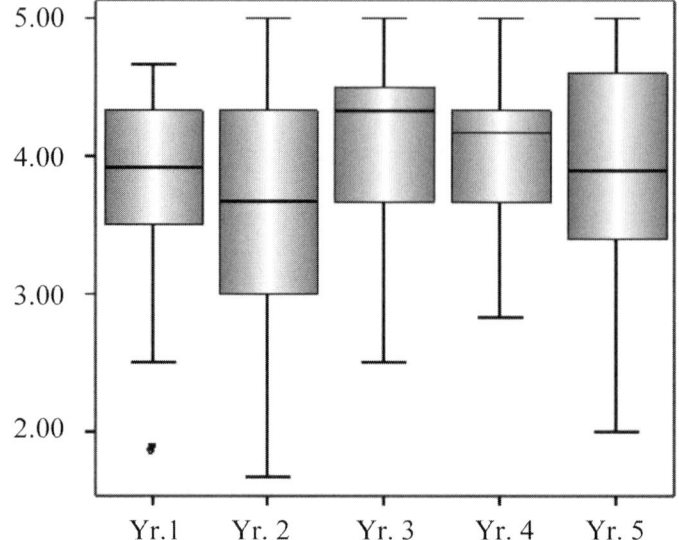

FIGURE 56.

ALL FIVE YEARS

SENIOR STUDENT PERFORMANCE DATA ACROSS FIVE YEARS

CRITERION 5: RHYTHM

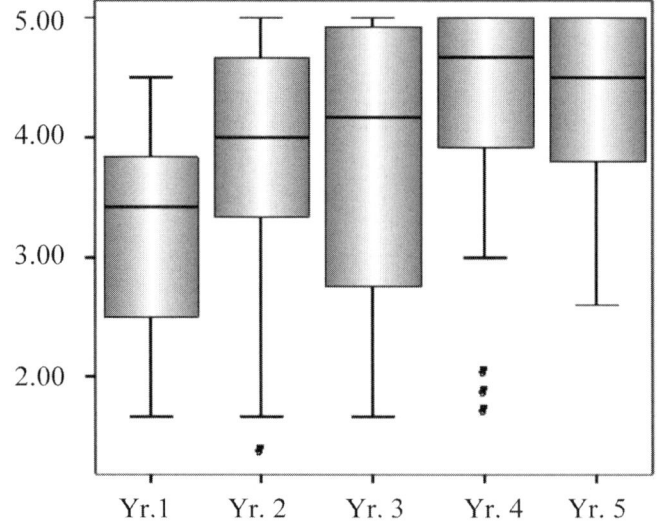

FIGURE 57.

ALL FIVE YEARS

SENIOR STUDENT PERFORMANCE DATA ACROSS FIVE YEARS

CRITERION 6: SCALES/TRIADS

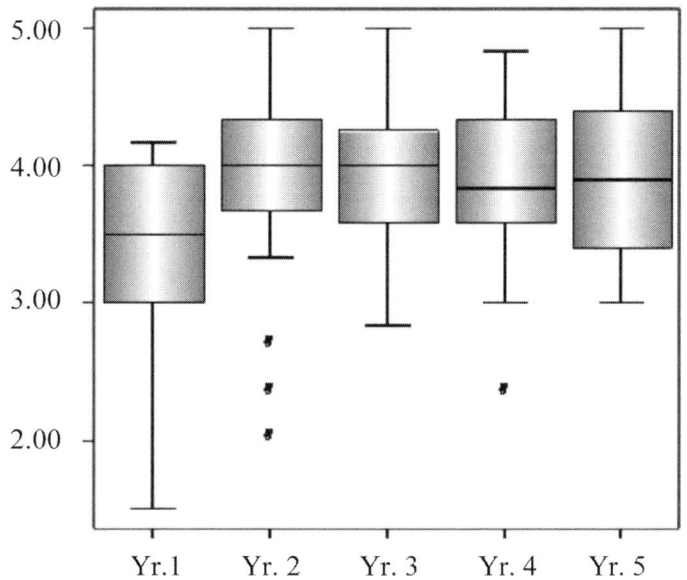

FIGURE 58.

ALL FIVE YEARS

SENIOR STUDENT PERFORMANCE DATA ACROSS FIVE YEARS

CRITERION 7: TECHNIQUE

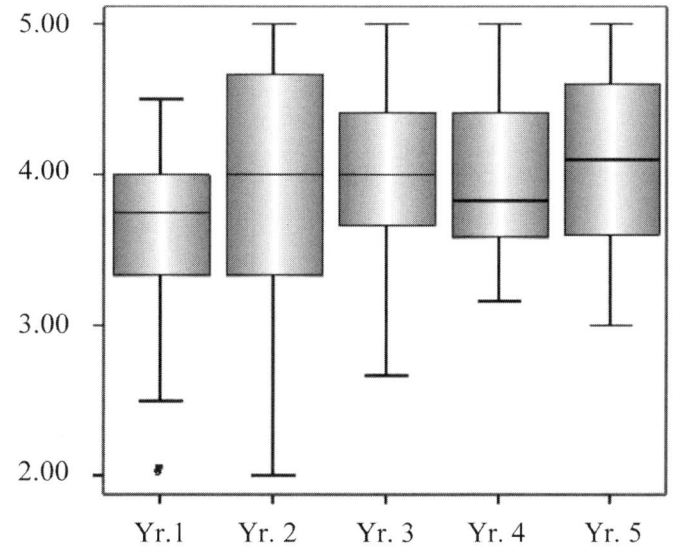

FIGURE 59.

ALL FIVE YEARS

SENIOR STUDENT PERFORMANCE DATA ACROSS FIVE YEARS

CRITERION 8: TONE QUALITY

PART TWO: MAY JURY AND SOLO CONTEST DATA FOR YEARS 1–4

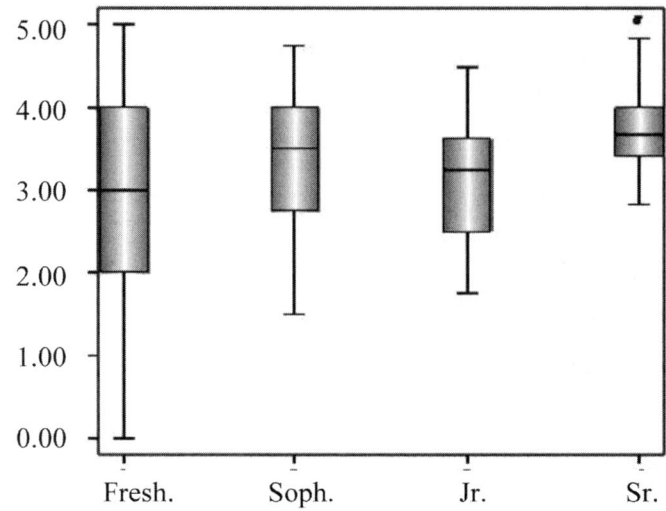

FIGURE 60.

CRITERION 1: DICTION, BOWING, AND ARTICULATION

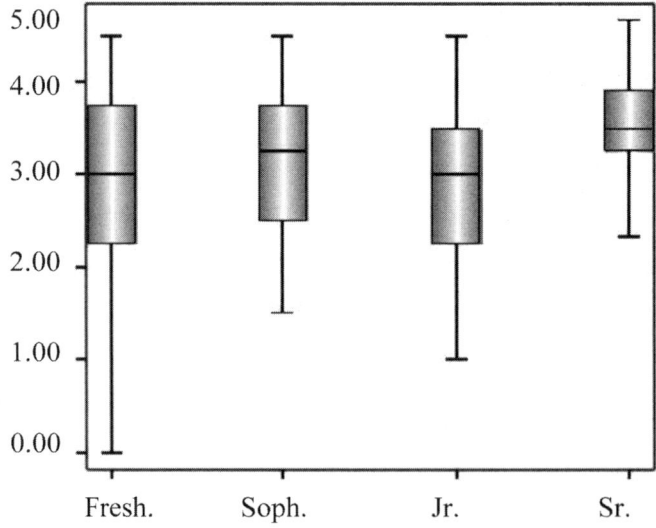

FIGURE 61.

CRITERION 2: INTERPRETATION AND MUSICIANSHIP

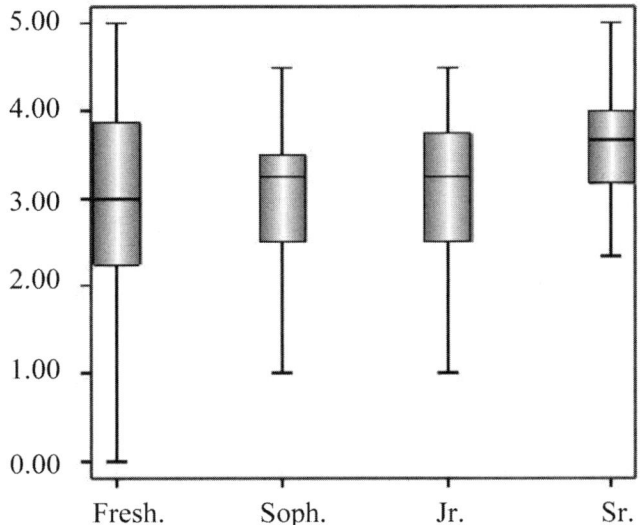

FIGURE 62.
CRITERION 3: INTONATION

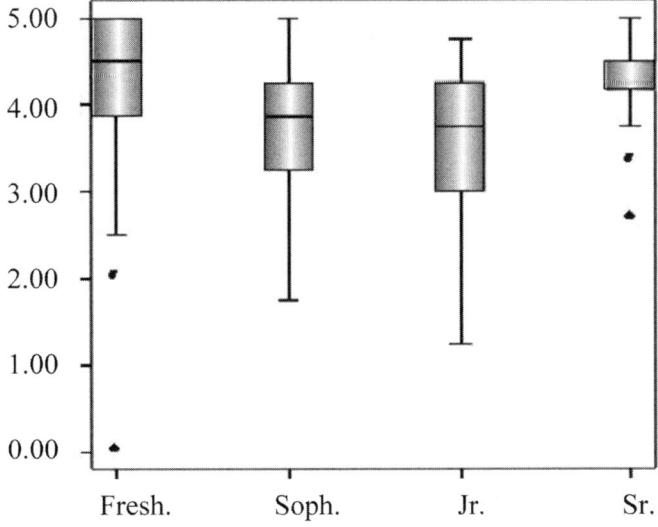

FIGURE 63.
CRITERION 4: PERFORMANCE FACTORS

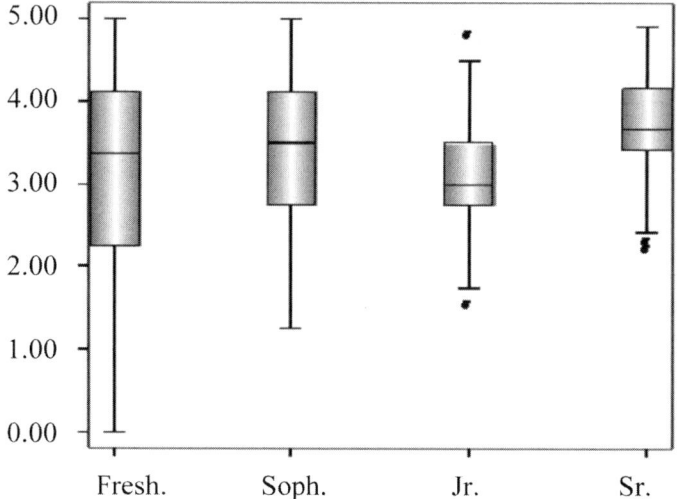

FIGURE 64.

CRITERION 5: RHYTHM

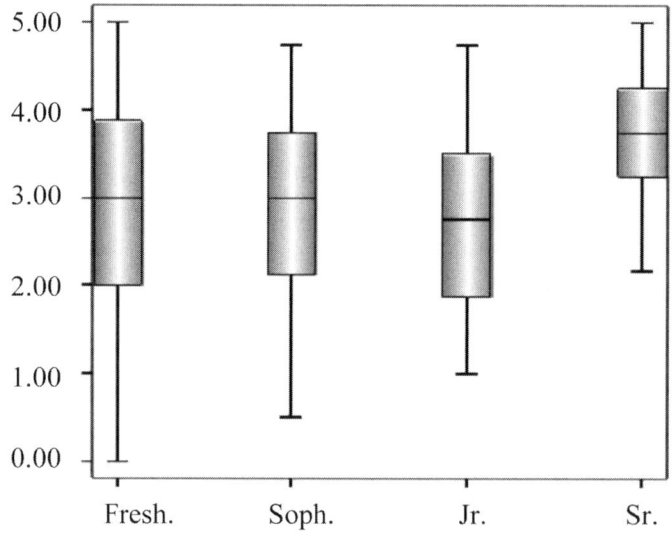

FIGURE 65.

CRITERION 6: SCALES AND TRIADS

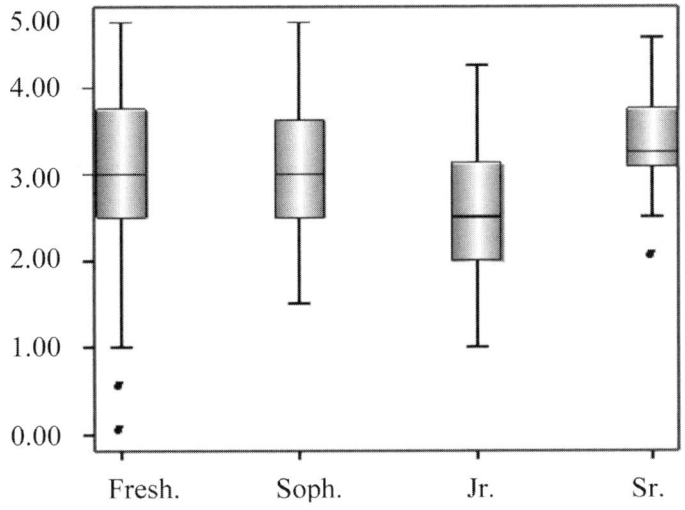

FIGURE 66.

CRITERION 7: TECHNIQUE

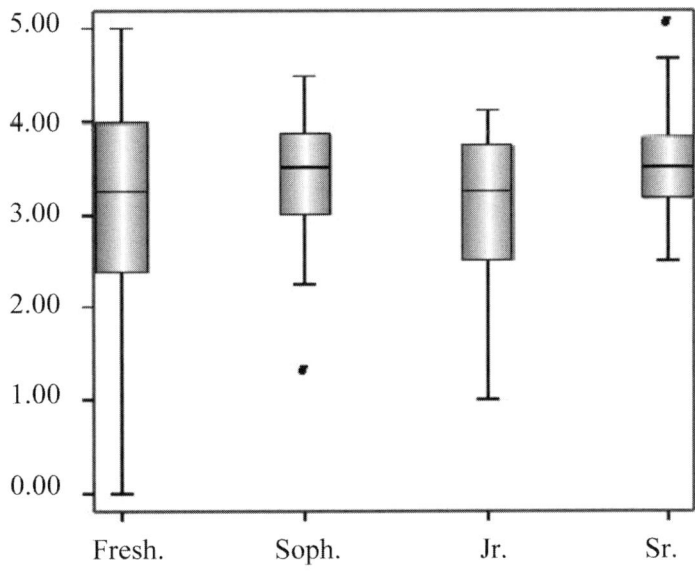

FIGURE 67.

CRITERION 8: TONE QUALITY

SUMMARY

The hard work and dedication you have shown by getting to this stage is amazing. You have transformed your students, parents, administrators, and more importantly, yourself. The educational atmosphere of your music department should be one in which your faculty is truly developing young people who understand that learning takes reflection and action based on information (data). Thinking of learning over a limited time has helped you to see and understand time as a valuable commodity that can't be wasted. Data has shown you how to use your time to make the most of learning situations. Congratulations on completing the eight steps in *Scale Your Way to Music Assessment*.

We hope you will visit our website (www.mpae.net) and share with us and others how your journey is going. Let us congratulate you and give you feedback as you develop an assessment plan.

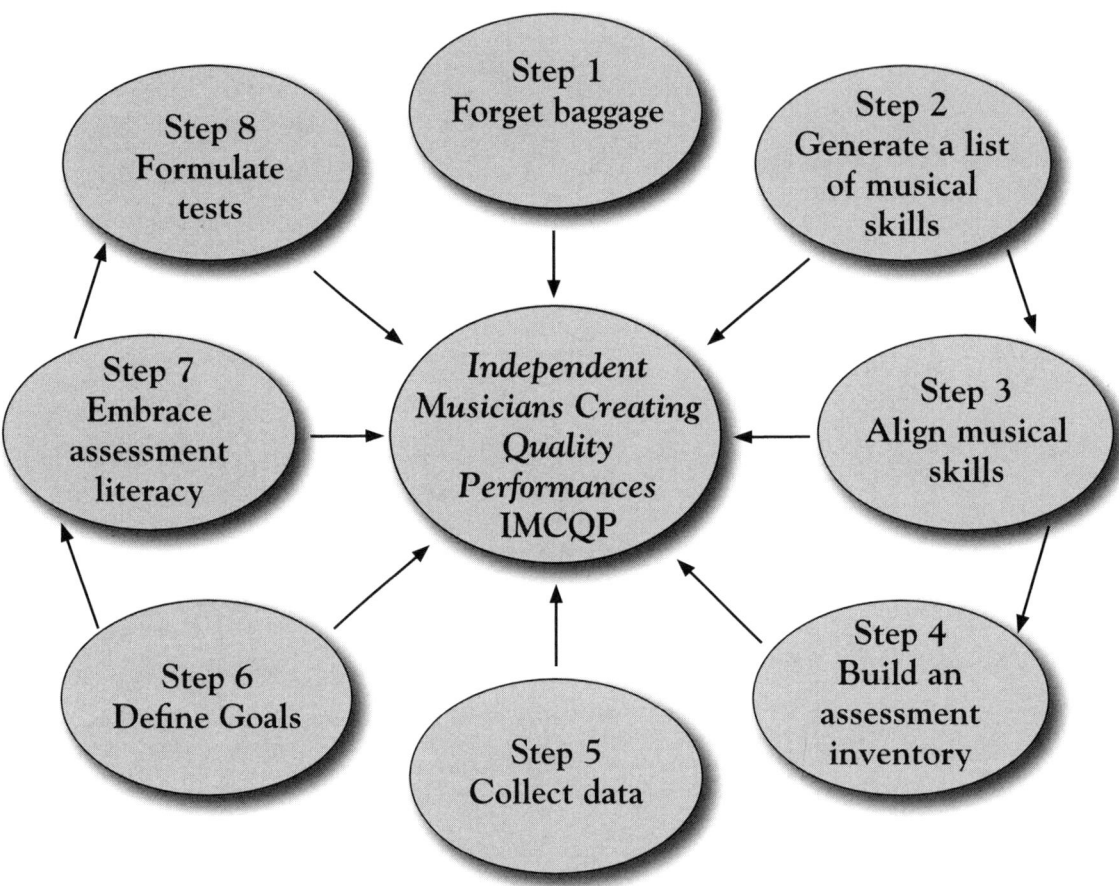

FIGURE 68.

CHAPTER 10

FINALE

LET US BEGIN

> Yesterday is gone. Tomorrow has not yet come.
> We have only today. Let us begin.
>
> *Mother Teresa (1910–1997)*
> *Missionary and winner of the Nobel Peace Prize*

We hope you look at the work you have done and are able to see the long-term benefits of using assessment to improve your teaching and your students' ability to become Independent Musicians Creating Quality Performances.

Now you know:

- that assessment is here to stay
- what musicians need to be able to do to be productive members of musical groups
- that state and national standards for music exist
- that the clock is ticking on the arts and its continued place in the schools
- that we are not leading assessment for the arts but are ignoring it
- that you must assess students every day
- how to collect formalized data to use to improve instruction

And finally, you know the steps, process, and reasons, and have the tools to create assessments.

In order to reach the goal of assessment, we as music educators need to change the way we see our profession and develop a community of learners who are committed to transforming our profession. As a community of learners, we will be able to touch the minds of students, teachers, and parents, and develop performance skills that will allow students to become Independent Musicians Creating Quality Performances that capture the ears and emotions of their audiences. We have seen the impact that creating quality assessments of performance can have on the students and music educators. By developing a music education culture that is not afraid to make the changes needed in the classroom, we will develop a community of learners who will support and continue this great profession. We have also seen students, staff, and administrations embrace a set of standards and strive to achieve them in ways not thought possible five years ago. These people are true believers in the power of knowledge and performance. Begin building your own community of education leaders and enjoy the excitement and thrill of taking the performance arts to the next level.

Knowing is doing. You have started your journey.

We congratulate you on taking what we have presented and using assessment to improve instruction. You have taken the information and adapted it to your situation. You have become a leader of assessment so that core curriculum teachers, your administrators, music staff, parents, and students see that music is a viable, measurable, and vital part of the school, community, and society. The time and energy you have spent developing your assessment program will help your music program flourish in the future by developing Independent Musicians Creating Quality Performances (IMCQP) who are well educated in performance, theory, and music appreciation. We commend you for creating the young people who are our future supporters and consumers of a very precious art form; they are our legacy for the future.

Your journey has begun!

FIGURE 69.

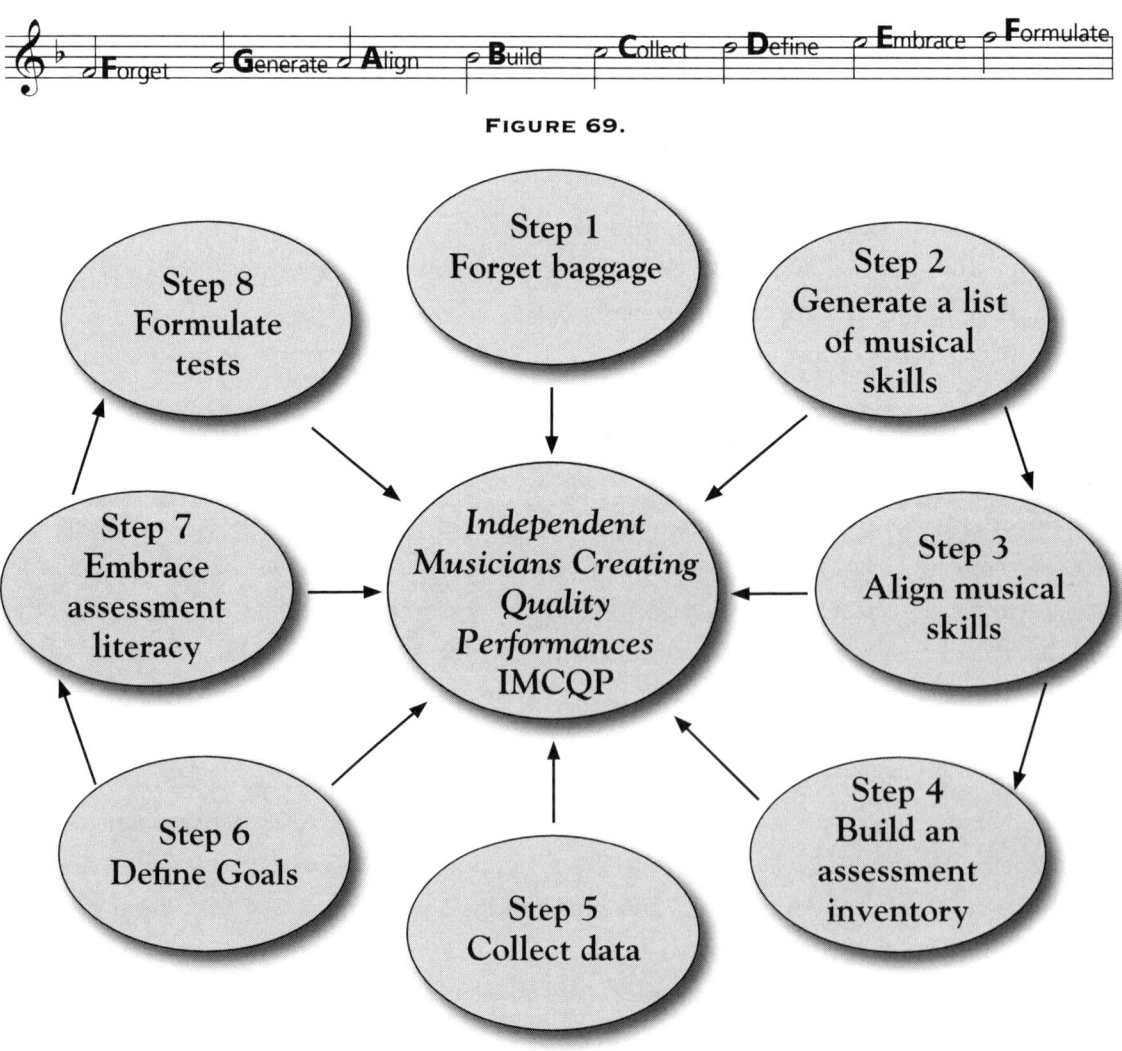

FIGURE 70.

APPENDIX A
TESTS FOR BAND

First-Year Band

Perform individual solo at contest or in front of band for rating or grade (required).

Perform in a small group (ensemble) at contest for rating (required).

Perform individual solo (see list), sightread and play/sing major and minor scales and triads (all forms) (for May jury).

Perform scales (concert pitch): C, F, B-flat, E-flat, A-flat, D-flat, G-flat, G, and D; sing C, F, and G.

Perform all three forms of minor scales: natural, harmonic, and melodic in keys listed above.

Play and sing major, minor, augmented, and diminished triads in keys listed above.

Sightread (singing and playing) rhythms and rests (see list).

Sightread (singing and playing) in these meters: 4/4, 3/4, and 2/4.

Year 1 Written Final

Volume 1, Unit 1	Staff, notes, and pitches
Volume 1, Unit 2	Note values, time signatures, and rests
Volume 1, Unit 3	Time signatures, ties, and slurs
Volume 1, Unit 4	Repeats, eighth notes, and dotted-quarter notes
Volume 1, Unit 5	Dynamics, tempo marks, articulations, D. C. and D. S. repeats
Volume 1, Unit 6	Flats, sharps, naturals, whole and half steps, enharmonics
Volume 2, Unit 7	Tetrachords, scales, and key signatures
Volume 2, Unit 8	Key signatures, chromatic scale, and intervals
Volume 2, Unit 9	Intervals and solfège

Year 1 Listening Final

Interval Recognition	Visual (ascending only)
Correct Notation	Listening
Rhythm and notes	
Rhythm	Visual
Scale recognition	Visual and listening
Intervals	Not visual
Triads	Not visual
Intervals	Visual

Second-Year Band

Perform individual solo at contest or in front of band for rating, comments, or grade (required).

Perform in a small group (ensemble) at contest for rating (required).

Perform individual solo (see list), sightread and play/sing major and minor scales and triads (all forms) (for May jury).

Play IMEA scales and (concert pitch) C, F, B-flat, E-flat, A-flat, D-flat, G-flat, G, and D.

Perform all three forms of minor scales: natural, harmonic, and melodic in keys listed above.

Play and sing major, minor, and diminished triads in these keys: C, F, B-flat, E-flat, A-flat, D-flat, G-flat, G, and D.

Sightread (singing and playing) rhythms and rests (see list).

Sightread (singing and playing) compound meters.

Year 2 Written Final

Volume 1, Unit 1	Staff, notes, and pitches
Volume 1, Unit 6	Flats, sharps, naturals, whole and half steps, and enharmonics
Volume 2, Unit 8	Key signatures, chromatic scale, and intervals
Volume 2, Unit 9	Intervals and solfège
Terms, goal setting	

Year 2 Listening Final

Interval recognition	Visual (ascending only)
Correct notation	Listening/visual
Rhythm and notes	Listening/visual
Rhythm	Listening/visual
Scale recognition	Listening/visual
Intervals	Not visual/listening
Triads	Not visual/listening
Intervals	No listening/visual only

Third-Year Band

Perform individual solo at contest or in front of band for rating, comments, or grade (required).

Perform in a small group (ensemble) at contest for rating (required).

Perform individual solo (see list), sightread and play/sing major and minor scales and triads (all forms) (for May jury).

Play IMEA scales and (concert pitch) C, F, B-flat, E-flat, A-flat, D-flat, G-flat, G, and D.

Perform all three forms of minor scales: natural, harmonic, and melodic in keys listed above.

Sightread (singing and playing) major, minor, and diminished triads in these keys: C, F, B-flat, E-flat, A-flat, D-flat, G-flat, G, and D.

Sightread (singing and playing) rhythms and rests (see list).

Sightread (singing and playing) compound meters.

Year 3 Written Final

Volume 1, Unit 1	The staff, notes, and pitches
Volume 1, Unit 3	Time signature, ties, and slurs
Volume 1, Unit 4	Repeats, eighth notes, and dotted-quarter notes
Volume 1, Unit 5	Dynamics, tempo marks, articulations, D. C. and D. S. repeats
Volume 2, Unit 7	Scales, key signatures
Volume 2, Unit 8	Chromatic scale and intervals
Volume 2, Unit 9	Intervals continued and solfège
Volume 2, Unit 10	Sixteenth notes, dotted-eighth notes, common and cut time
Volume 2, Unit 11	3/8 and 6/8 time signatures, triplets, and syncopation
Volume 3, Unit 14	Minor scales and triads
Volume 3, Unit 18	Basic forms of music

Year 3 Listening Final

Interval recognition	Visual (ascending and descending)
Correct notation	Listening
Rhythm and notes	
Melodic pitch recognition	
Scale recognition	Visual
Intervals	Not visual
Triads	Not visual
Scales recognition	Not visual

Fourth-Year Band

Perform individual solo at contest or in front of band for rating, comments, or grade (required).

Perform in a small group (ensemble) at contest for rating (required).

Perform individual solo (see list), sightread and play/sing major and minor scales and triads (all forms) (in May jury).

Perform playing IMEA scales and (concert pitch): C, F, B-flat, E-flat, A-flat, D-flat, G-flat, G, and D.

Perform all three forms of minor scales: natural, harmonic, and melodic in keys listed above.

Play and sing major, minor, and diminished triads in these keys: C, F, B-flat, E-flat, A-flat, D-flat, G-flat, G, and D.

Sightread (singing and playing) rhythms and rests (see list).

Sightread (singing and playing) compound meters.

Year 4 Written Final

Volume 2, Unit 7	Scales and key signatures
Volume 2, Unit 8	Chromatic scale and intervals
Volume 2, Unit 9	Intervals and solfège
Volume 2, Unit 10	Sixteenth notes, dotted notes and cut time
Volume 2, Unit 11	3/8 and 6/8 time signatures, triplets, and syncopation
Volume 2, Unit 12	Triads
Volume 3, Unit 13	Triads and inversions
Volume 3, Unit 14	Minor scales and triads
Volume 3, Unit 15	Chord progressions
Volume 3, Unit 18	Forms of music

Year 4 Listening Final

Interval recognition	Visual (ascending and descending)
Tetrachords	
Rhythm and notes	
Melodic pitch recognition	
Scale recognition	Visual
Triads	Visual
Intervals	Not visual
Triads	Not visual
Triads	Inversions
Scales	Not visual

APPENDIX B
TESTS FOR CHOIR

First Year Choir

Perform individual solo at contest for rating or comment (optional).

Perform in a small group (ensemble) at contest for rating or comment (required).

Perform solo in May (jury style).

Perform on piano and sing these scales: C, F, and G.

Play and sing major, minor, and diminished triads in C, F, and G.

Sightread at the piano.

Sightread (singing and playing) rhythms and rests (see list).

Sightread (singing and playing) in these meters: 4/4, 3/4, and 2/4.

Year 1 Written Final

Volume 1, Unit 1	Staff, notes, and pitches
Volume 1, Unit 2	Note values, time signatures, and rests
Volume 1, Unit 3	Time signatures, ties, and slurs
Volume 1, Unit 4	Repeats, eighth notes, and dotted-quarter notes
Volume 1, Unit 5	Dynamics, tempo marks, articulations, D. C. and D. S. repeats
Volume 1, Unit 6	Flats, sharps, naturals, whole and half steps, and enharmonics
Volume 2, Unit 7	Tetrachords, scales, and key signatures
Volume 2, Unit 8	Key signatures, chromatic scale, and intervals
Volume 2, Unit 9	Intervals and solfège

Year 1 Listening Final

Interval recognition	Visual (ascending only)
Correct notation	Listening
Rhythm and Notes	
Rhythm	Visual
Scale recognition	Visual and listening
Intervals	Not visual
Triads	Not visual
Intervals	Visual

Second Year Choir

Perform individual solo at contest for rating or comment (optional).

Perform in a small group (ensemble) at contest for rating or comment (required).

Perform solo in May (jury style).

Perform on piano and sing these scales: major, natural, harmonic, and melodic minor in C, G, D, F, and B-flat.

Play and sing major, minor, and diminished triads in C, G, D, F, and B-flat.

Sightread at the piano.

Sightread (singing and playing) rhythms and rests (see list).

Sightread (singing and playing) compound meters.

Year 2 Written Final

Volume 1, Unit 1	Staff, notes, and pitches
Volume 1, Unit 6	Flats, sharps, naturals, whole and half steps, and enharmonics
Volume 2, Unit 8	Key signatures, chromatic scale, and intervals
Volume 2, Unit 9	Intervals and solfège
Terms, goal setting	

Year 2 Listening Final

Interval recognition	Visual (ascending only)
Correct notation	Listening and visual
Rhythm and notes	Listening and visual
Rhythm	Listening and visual
Scale recognition	Listening and visual
Intervals	Not visual and listening
Triads	Not visual and listening
Intervals	No listening/visual only

Third Year Choir

Perform individual solo at contest for rating or comment (required).

Perform in a small group (ensemble) at contest for rating or comment (required).

Perform solo in May (jury style).

Perform on piano and sing these scales: C, G, D, A, F, B-flat, and E-flat.

Play and sing these scales: major, natural, harmonic, and melodic minor: C, G, D, A, F, B-flat, and E-flat.

Play and sing major, minor, and diminished triads in C, G, D, A, F, B-flat, and E-flat.

Sightread at the piano.

Sightread (singing and playing) rhythms and rests (see list).

Sightread (singing and playing) compound meters.

Year 3 Written Test

Volume 1, Unit 1	Staff, notes, and pitches
Volume 1, Unit 3	Time signatures, ties, and slurs
Volume 1, Unit 4	Repeats, eighth notes, and dotted-quarter notes
Volume 1, Unit 5	Dynamics, tempo marks, articulations, D. C. and D. S. repeats
Volume 2, Unit 7	Scales and key signatures
Volume 2, Unit 8	Chromatic scale and intervals
Volume 2, Unit 9	Intervals continued and solfège
Volume 2, Unit 10	Sixteenth notes, dotted-eighth notes, and common and cut time
Volume 2, Unit 11	3/8 and 6/8 time signatures, triplets, and syncopation
Volume 3, Unit 14	Minor scales and triads
Volume 3, Unit 18	Basic forms of music

Year 3 Listening Final

Interval recognition	Visual (ascending and descending)
Correct notation	Listening
Rhythm and notes	
Melodic pitch recognition	
Scale recognition	Visual
Intervals	Not visual
Triads	Not visual
Scales recognition	Not visual

Fourth Year Choir

Perform individual solo at contest for rating or comment (required).

Perform solo in May (jury style).

Perform in a small group (ensemble) at contest for rating or comment (required).

Perform on piano and sing these scales: major, natural, harmonic, and melodic minor in C, G, D, A, F, B-flat, and E-flat.

Play and sing major, minor, and diminished triads in C, G, D, A, F, B-flat, and E-flat.

Sightread at the piano,

Sightread (singing and playing) rhythms and rests (see list).

Year 4 Written Final

Volume 2, Unit 7	Scales and key signatures
Volume 2, Unit 8	Chromatic scale and intervals
Volume 2, Unit 9	Intervals and solfège
Volume 2, Unit 10	Sixteenth notes, dotted notes, and cut time
Volume 2, Unit 11	3/8 and 6/8 time signatures, triplets, and syncopation
Volume 2, Unit 12	Triads
Volume 3, Unit 13	Triads and inversions
Volume 3, Unit 14	Minor scales and triads
Volume 3, Unit 15	Chord progressions
Volume 3, Unit 18	Forms of music

Year 4 Listening Final

Interval recognition	Visual (ascending and descending)
Tetrachords	
Rhythm and notes	
Melodic pitch recognition	
Scale recognition	Visual
Triads	Visual
Intervals	Not visual
Triads	Not visual
Triads	Inversions
Scales	Not visual

APPENDIX C
TESTS FOR ORCHESTRA

First Year Orchestra

Perform individual solo at contest or in front of orchestra for rating, comments, or grade (optional).

Perform in a small group (ensemble) at contest for rating (required).

Perform individual etude (see list), major and minor scales and triads (all forms) (sing/play) in May (jury).

Perform these major, natural, harmonic, and melodic minors scales: C, F, G, D, A, and E. Play and sing major, minor, and diminished triads in C, F, and G.

Sightread.

Sightread (singing and playing) rhythms and rests (see list).

Sightread (singing and playing) 4/4, 3/4, and 2/4 meters.

Year 1 Written Final

Volume 1, Unit 1	Staff, notes, and pitches
Volume 1, Unit 2	Note values, time signatures, and rests
Volume 1, Unit 3	Time signatures, ties, and slurs
Volume 1, Unit 4	Repeats, eighth notes, and dotted-quarter notes
Volume 1, Unit 5	Dynamics, tempo marks, articulations, D. C. and D. S. repeats
Volume 1, Unit 6	Flats, sharps, naturals, whole and half steps, and enharmonics
Volume 2, Unit 7	Tetrachords, scales, and key signatures
Volume 2, Unit 8	Key signatures, chromatic scale, and intervals
Volume 2, Unit 9	Intervals and solfège

Year 1 Listening Final

Interval recognition	Visual (ascending only)
Correct notation	Listening
Rhythm and notes	
Rhythm	Visual
Scale recognition	Visual and listening
Intervals	Not visual
Triads	Not visual
Intervals	Visual

Second Year Orchestra

Perform individual solo at contest or in front of orchestra for rating, comments, or grade (required).

Perform in a small group (ensemble) at contest for rating (required).

Perform individual solo (see list), scales, and triads (sing/play) in May (jury).

Perform major, natural, harmonic, and melodic minors scales: C, F, G, D, A, and E.

Play and sing major, minor, augmented, and diminished triads in these keys: C, F, and G.

Sightread.

Sightread (singing and playing) rhythms and rests (see list).

Sightread (singing and playing) compound meters.

Year 2 Written Final

Volume 1, Unit 1	Staff, notes, and pitches
Volume 1, Unit 6	Flats, sharps, naturals, whole and half steps, and enharmonics
Volume 2, Unit 8	Key signatures, chromatic scale, and intervals
Volume 2, Unit 9	Intervals and solfège
Terms, goal setting	

Year 2 Listening Final

Interval recognition	Visual (ascending only)
Correct notation	Listening and visual
Rhythm and notes	Listening and visual
Rhythm	Listening and visual
Scale recognition	Listening and visual
Intervals	Not visual and listening
Triads	Not visual and listening
Intervals	No listening/visual only

Third Year Orchestra

Perform individual solo at contest or in front of orchestra for rating, comments, or grade (required).

Perform in a small group (ensemble) at contest for rating (required).

Perform individual solo (see list), scales, and triads (sing/play) in May (jury).

Perform major, natural, harmonic, and melodic minor scales: C, F, G, D, A, and E.

Play and sing major, minor, and diminished triads in these keys: C, F, G, D, A, and E.

Sightread.

Sightread (singing and playing) rhythms and rests (see list).

Sightread (singing and playing) compound meters.

Year 3 Written Final

Volume 1, Unit 1	Staff, notes, and pitches
Volume 1, Unit 3	Time signatures, ties, and slurs
Volume 1, Unit 4	Repeats, eighth notes, and dotted-quarter notes
Volume 1, Unit 5	Dynamics, tempo marks, articulations, D. C. and D. S. repeats
Volume 2, Unit 7	Scales and key signatures
Volume 2, Unit 8	Chromatic scale and intervals
Volume 2, Unit 9	Intervals continued and solfège
Volume 2, Unit 10	Sixteenth notes, dotted-eighth notes, and common and cut time
Volume 2, Unit 11	3/8 and 6/8 time signatures, triplets, and syncopation
Volume 3, Unit 14	Minor scales and triads
Volume 3, Unit 18	Basic forms of music

Year 3 Listening Final

Interval recognition	Visual (ascending and descending)
Correct notation	Listening
Rhythm and notes	
Melodic pitch recognition	
Scale recognition	Visual
Intervals	Not visual
Triads	Not visual
Scales recognition	Not visual

Fourth Year Orchestra

Perform individual solo at contest or in front of orchestra for rating, comments, or grade (required).

Perform in May (jury style).

Perform in a small group (ensemble) at contest for rating (required).

Perform major, natural, harmonic, and melodic minor scales: C, F, G, D, A, and E.

Play and sing major, minor, and diminished triads in these keys: C, F, G, D, A, and E.

Sightread.

Sightread (singing and playing) rhythms and rests (see list).

Year 4 Written Final

Volume 2, Unit 7	Scales and key signatures
Volume 2, Unit 8	Chromatic scale and intervals
Volume 2, Unit 9	Intervals and solfège
Volume 2, Unit 10	Sixteenth notes, dotted notes, and cut time
Volume 2, Unit 11	3/8 and 6/8 time signatures, triplets, and syncopation
Volume 2, Unit 12	Triads
Volume 3, Unit 13	Triads and inversions
Volume 3, Unit 14	Minor scales and triads
Volume 3, Unit 15	Chord progressions
Volume 3, Unit 18	Forms of music

Year 4 Listening Final

Interval recognition	Visual (ascending and descending)
Tetrachords	
Rhythm and notes	
Melodic pitch recognition	
Scale recognition	Visual
Triads	Visual
Intervals	Not visual
Triads	Not visual
Triads	Inversions
Scales	Not visual

APPENDIX D
YEAR 1 WRITTEN TEST

Name_____

Class _____

1. A–C–E–G are the names of the spaces for which clef?

2. F–A–C–E are the names of the spaces of which clef?

3. G–B–D–F–A are the names of the lines for which clef?

4. E–G–B–D–F are the names of the lines in which clef?

5. In this example a ♭ sign:
    A. Raises
    B. Lowers
    C. Cancels
    D. Does nothing

6. In this example a ♮ sign:
    A. Raises
    B. Lowers
    C. Cancels
    D. Does nothing

7. In this example a ♯ sign:
   A. Raises
   B. Lowers
   C. Cancels
   D. Does nothing

8. Based on the key, a ♮ sign:
   A. Raises
   B. Lowers
   C. Cancels
   D. Does nothing

9. Which bar has the sharps in the correct order?

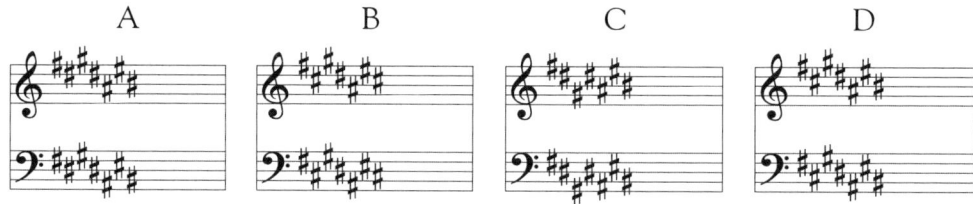

10. Which bar has the flats in the correct order?

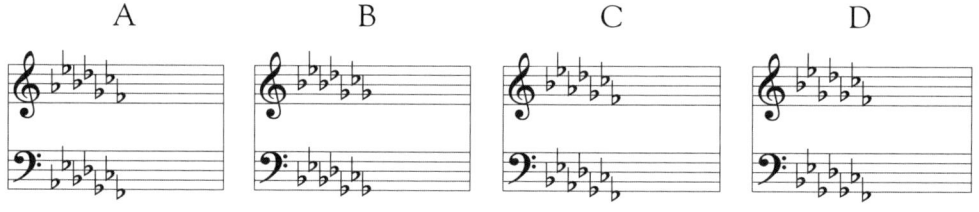

11. Which example is a tetrachord?

12. What is the pattern of whole (W) and half (H) steps in a major scale?
    A. W–H–W–W–W–H–W
    B. W–W–W–H–W–W–H
    C. W–W–H–W–H–W–H
    D. W–W–H–W–W–W–H

13. Which example is a major scale?

A   B   C   D

14. Which example is a major scale?

A   B   C   D

15. The space between two notes is called a(n):
    A. Chord
    B. Interval
    C. Tetrachord
    D. Arpeggio

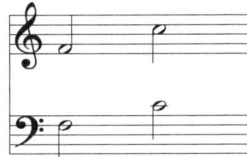

16. The interval shown is a:
    A. Second
    B. Third
    C. Fifth
    D. Sixth

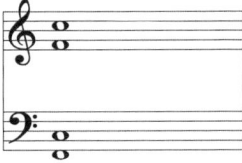

17. The interval shown is a:
    A. Fourth
    B. Third
    C. Second
    D. Fifth

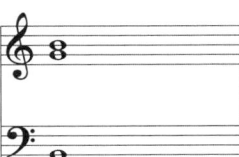

18. The interval shown is a:
    A. Sixth
    B. Fourth
    C. Seventh
    D. Fifth

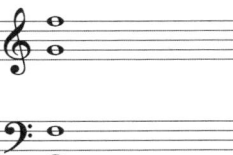

19. The interval shown is a:
    A. Sixth
    B. Fifth
    C. Seventh
    D. Fourth

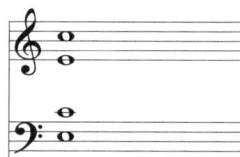

20. The interval shown is a:
    A. Third
    B. Second
    C. Fourth
    D. Fifth

21. In a major scale, all of the intervals are either:
    A. Minor and major
    B. Major and perfect
    C. Perfect and minor
    D. Major and augmented

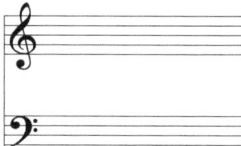

22. Based on the key signature, the interval shown is a:
    A. Perfect fifth
    B. Minor sixth
    C. Major seventh
    D. Major sixth

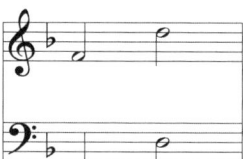

23. Based on the key signature, the interval shown is a:
    A. Minor third
    B. Perfect fourth
    C. Major third
    D. Major second

24. Based on the key signature, the interval shown is a:
    A. Major seventh
    B. Minor seventh
    C. Major sixth
    D. Minor sixth

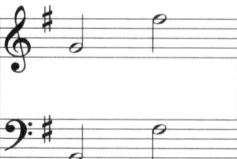

25. Based on the key signature, the interval shown is a:
    A. Perfect fourth
    B. Tritone
    C. Perfect fifth
    D. Augmented fourth

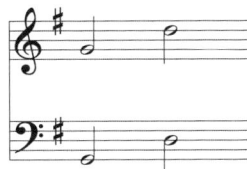

26. Based on the key signature, the interval shown is a(n):
    A. Octave
    B. Minor seventh
    C. Major seventh
    D. Major sixth

27. Notes outside of a key are:
    A. Major, diminished, and augmented
    B. Augmented, minor, and major
    C. Augmented, diminished, and minor
    D. Augmented, diminished, and major

28. Based on the key signature, the interval shown is a:
    A. Minor seventh
    B. Major seventh
    C. Minor sixth
    D. Major sixth

29. Based on the key signature, the interval shown is a:
    A. Minor second
    B. Major third
    C. Major second
    D. Minor third

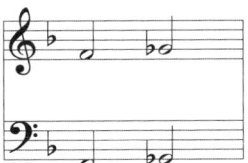

30. Based on the key signature, the interval shown is a:
    A. Minor second
    B. Major third
    C. Major second
    D. Minor third

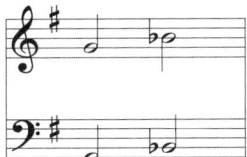

31. Based on the key signature, the interval shown is a:
    A. Perfect fifth
    B. Perfect fourth
    C. Diminished fifth
    D. Diminished fourth

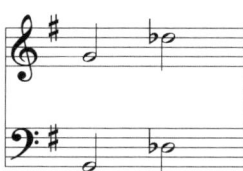

32. Based on the key signature, the interval shown is a:
    A. Perfect fifth
    B. Major third
    C. Perfect fourth
    D. Augmented fourth

33. Based on the key signature, the interval shown is a:
    A. Major seventh
    B. Major sixth
    C. Minor sixth
    D. Minor seventh

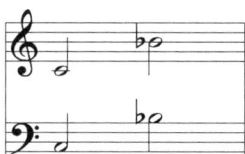

34. Based on the key signature, the interval shown is a:
    A. Perfect fourth
    B. Minor third
    C. Major third
    D. Diminished fourth

35. A major triad is made up of which two thirds?
    A. Minor bottom and major top
    B. Minor bottom and minor top
    C. Major bottom and minor top
    D. Major bottom and major top

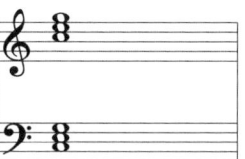

36. A minor triad is made up of which two thirds?
    A. Minor bottom and major top
    B. Minor bottom and minor top
    C. Major bottom and minor top
    D. Major bottom and major top

37. A diminished triad is made up of which two thirds?
    A. Minor bottom and major top
    B. Minor bottom and minor top
    C. Major bottom and minor top
    D. Major bottom and major top

38. An augmented triad is made up of which two thirds?
    A. Minor bottom and major top
    B. Minor bottom and minor top
    C. Major bottom and minor top
    D. Major bottom and major top

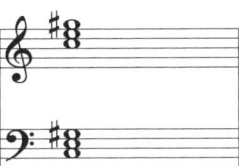

39. In a major key, the major triads are:
    A. I–ii–V
    B. I–IV–vi
    C. I–iii–V
    D. I–IV–V

40. In a major key, the minor triads are:
    A. ii–iii–V
    B. ii–iii–vi
    C. ii–iii–vii
    D. I–IV–V

41. In a major key, the diminished triad is:
    A. vi
    B. i
    C. vii
    D. v

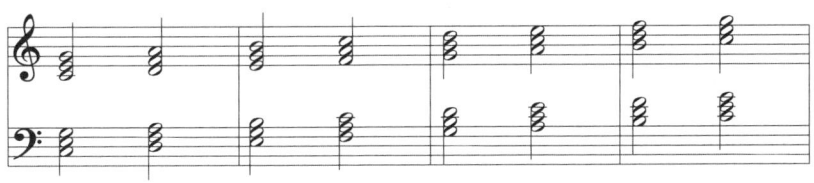

42. Based on the key, the triad shown is:
    A. Major
    B. Minor
    C. Diminished
    D. Augmented

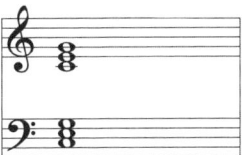

43. Based on the key, the triad shown is:
    A. Major
    B. Minor
    C. Diminished
    D. Augmented

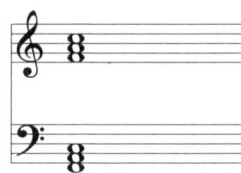

44. Based on the key, the triad shown is:
    A. Major
    B. Minor
    C. Diminished
    D. Augmented

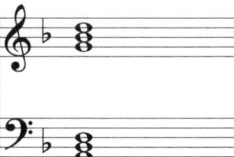

45. Based on the key, the triad shown is:
    A. Major
    B. Minor
    C. Diminished
    D. Augmented

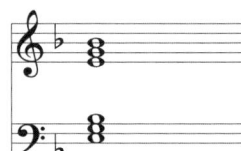

46. Name the key or scale that matches the key signature shown:
    A. B-flat
    B. E-flat
    C. F
    D. C

47. Name the key or scale that matches the key signature shown:
    A. D
    B. G
    C. F
    D. C

48. Name the key or scale that matches the key signature shown:
    A. D
    B. B-flat
    C. F
    D. E-flat

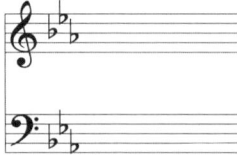

49. Name the key or scale that matches the key signature shown:
    A. D
    B. A
    C. F
    D. E

50. What scale would you use to play this melody?
    A. E natural minor
    B. G major
    C. E harmonic minor
    D. F-sharp major

51. What scale would you use to play this melody?
    A. E natural minor
    B. G major
    C. E harmonic minor
    D. F-sharp major

52. What scale would you use to play this melody?
    A. B natural minor
    B. G major
    C. B harmonic minor
    D. D major

53. 4/4 means:
    A. Four beats to the bar and the eighth note gets one beat
    B. Four beats to the bar and the quarter note gets two beats
    C. Four beats to the bar and the quarter note gets one beat
    D. Four beats to the bar and the half note gets one beat

54. 6/8 means:
    A. Six beats to the bar and the dotted-quarter note gets one beat
    B. Six beats to the bar and the eighth note gets two beats
    C. Six beats to the bar and the quarter note gets two beats
    D. Six beats to the bar and the eighth note gets one beat

55. Which example has moderately loud notation?

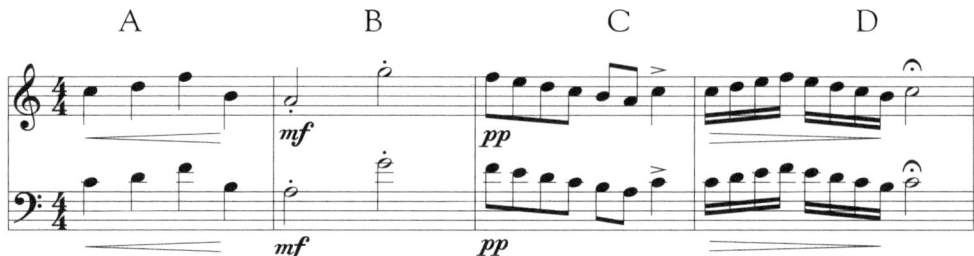

56. Which example has crescendo notation?

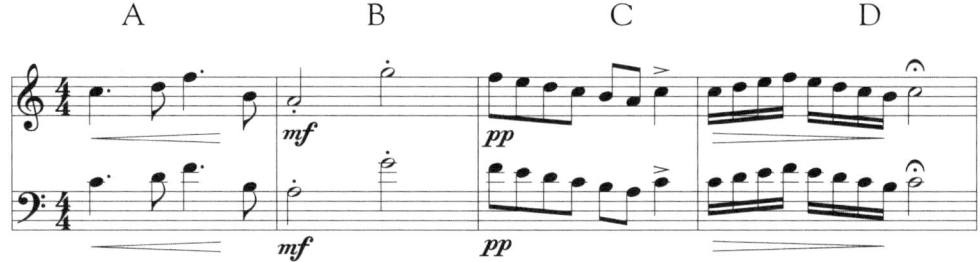

57. Which example has staccato notation?

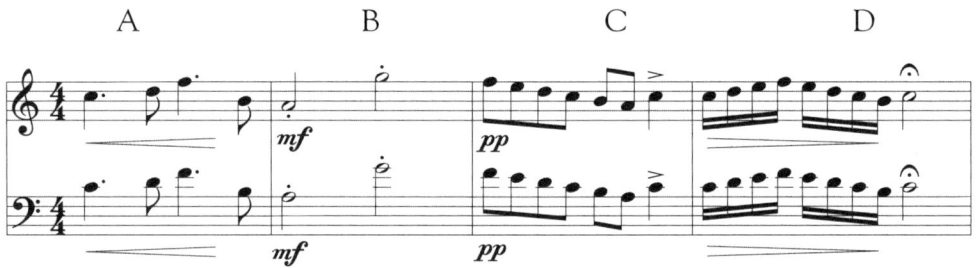

58. Which example has a fermata?

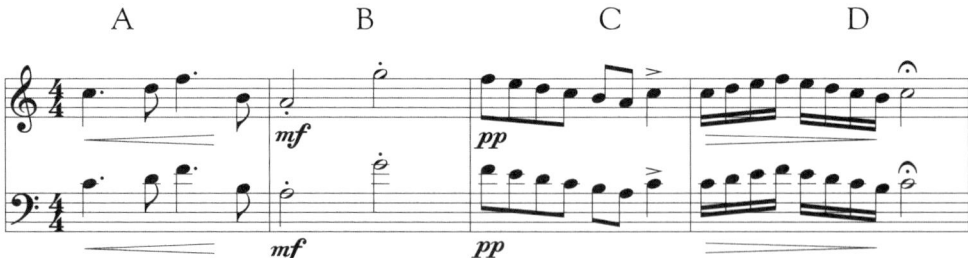

59. What is the enharmonic equivalent of the example?

A. G-flat
B. A
C. A-flat
D. F-sharp

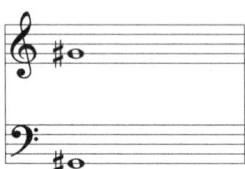

60. What is the enharmonic equivalent of the example?
    A. C-sharp
    B. D-flat
    C. E
    D. E-flat

61. What is the enharmonic equivalent of the example?
    A. D-sharp
    B. E-sharp
    C. G-flat
    D. E

62. What note is a whole step above the note shown?
    A. C
    B. C-sharp
    C. B-sharp
    D. B-flat

63. What note is a whole step above the note shown?
    A. A-flat
    B. G-sharp
    C. A
    D. G

64. What note is a half step above the note shown?
    A. E-flat
    B. D-flat
    C. F
    D. F-flat

65. What note is a half step above the note shown?
    A. D
    B. D-flat
    C. D-sharp
    D. C-flat

66. The minor key signature shown is:
    A. G minor
    B. A minor
    C. C minor
    D. B minor

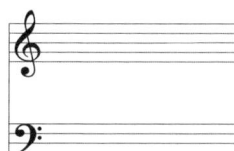

67. The minor key signature shown is:
    A. E minor
    B. F minor
    C. D minor
    D. D-sharp minor

68. The minor key signature shown is:
    A. G minor
    B. D minor
    C. B-flat minor
    D. G minor

69. Which tetrachord is correct?

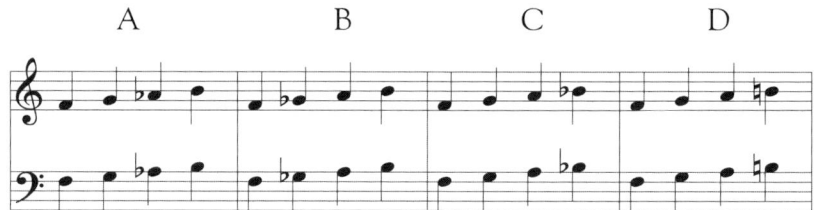

70. Which tetrachord is correct?

71. Which tetrachord is correct?

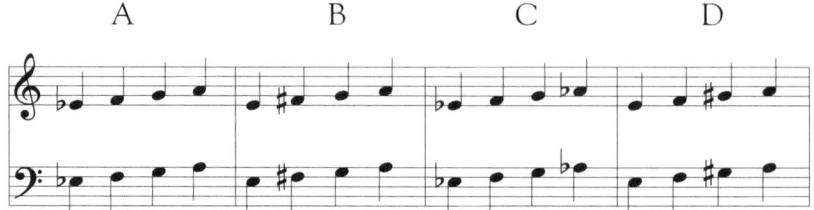

72. Which example is counted correctly?

73. Which example is counted correctly?

74. Which example is counted correctly?

75. Which example is counted correctly?

76. Which metronome marking is used with the term adagio in 4/4?

A. ♩ = 66–76

B. ♩ = 120–168

C. ♩ = 40–60

D. ♩ = 168–200

77. Which metronome marking is used with the term allegro in 4/4?

    A. ♩ = 66–76

    B. ♩ = 120–168

    C. ♩ = 40–60

    D. ♩ = 168–200

78. Which metronome marking is used with the term vivace in 4/4?

    A. ♩ = 66–76

    B. ♩ = 120–168

    C. ♩ = 40–60

    D. ♩ = 168–200

79. Which metronome marking is used with the term largo in 4/4?

    A. ♩ = 66–76

    B. ♩ = 120–168

    C. ♩ = 40–60

    D. ♩ = 168–200

80. Name the solfège symbol for the note indicated.

    A. Fa

    B. Re

    C. Mi

    D. Ti

81. Name the solfège symbol for the note indicated.

    A. Fa

    B. Re

    C. Mi

    D. So

82. Name the solfège symbol for the note indicated.

    A. La

    B. Re

    C. So

    D. Fa

83. Name the solfège symbol for the note indicated.
    A. Re
    B. Do
    C. Mi
    D. Fa

84. In music, *Fine* means:
    A. Repeat
    B. Everything is okay
    C. End
    D. Hold out

85. The term *a tempo* means:
    A. Gradually slow down
    B. Gradually speed up
    C. Return to original tempo
    D. Return to letter A

The NFHS music rubric uses a series of numeric and written descriptors to assess music performance. Questions 86–91 are based on the assessment form.

86. A rating of 3 is defined as:
    A. A good performance (lacking finesse and/or interpretation)
    B. A fair performance (basic weaknesses)
    C. An excellent performance (minor defects)
    D. A superior performance (outstanding in nearly every detail)

87. A rating of 4 is defined as:
    A. A good performance (lacking finesse and/or interpretation)
    B. A fair performance (basic weaknesses)
    C. An excellent performance (minor defects)
    D. A superior performance (outstanding in nearly every detail)

88. Style, phrasing, tempo, dynamics, and emotional involvement are terms used to describe:
    A. Diction, bowing, and/or articulation
    B. Interpretation and musicianship
    C. Tone quality
    D. Intonation

89. Artistry, attacks, releases, control of ranges, and musical and/or mechanical skill are terms used to describe:
    A. Diction, bowing, and/or articulation
    B. Interpretation and musicianship
    C. Tone quality
    D. Technique (facility and/or accuracy)

90. Resonance, control, claritry, focus, consistency, and warmth are terms used to describe:
    A. Diction, bowing, and/or articulation
    B. Interpretation and musicianship
    C. Tone quality
    D. Technique (facility and/or accuracy)

91. Accuracy of note and rest values, duration, pulse, steadiness, and correctness of meters are terms used to describe:
    A. Diction, bowing, and/or articulation
    B. Rhythm
    C. Tone quality
    D. Technique (facility and/or accuracy)

APPENDIX E
YEAR 1 LISTENING TEST

Name _____

Class _____

1. Which interval is being played?

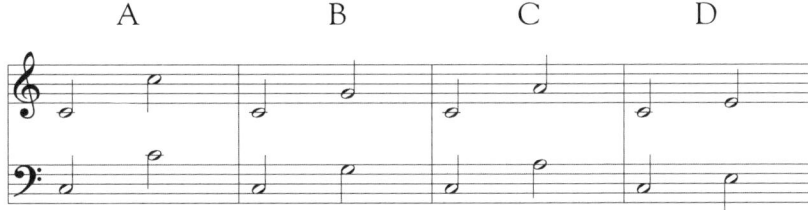

2. Which interval is being played?

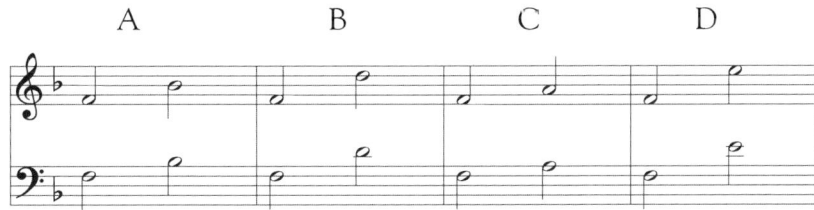

3. Which interval is being played?

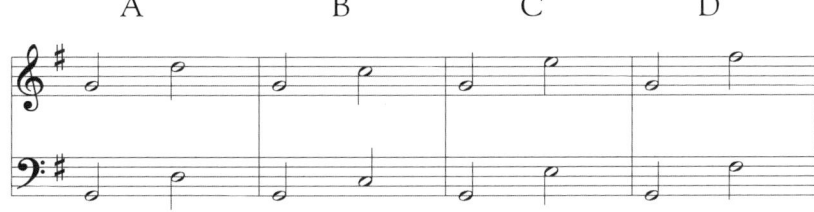

4. Which interval is being played?

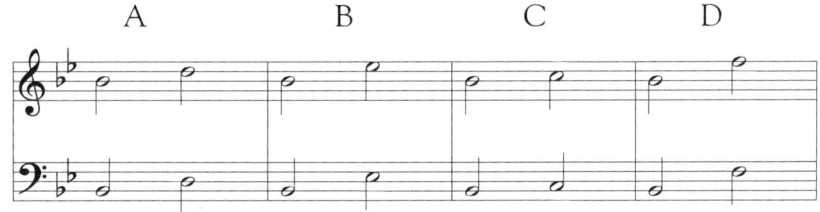

5. Which interval is being played?

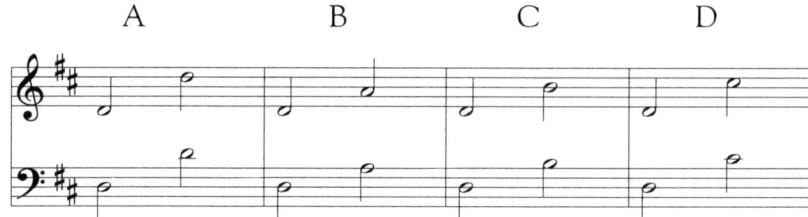

6. Which example is being played?

7. Which example is being played?

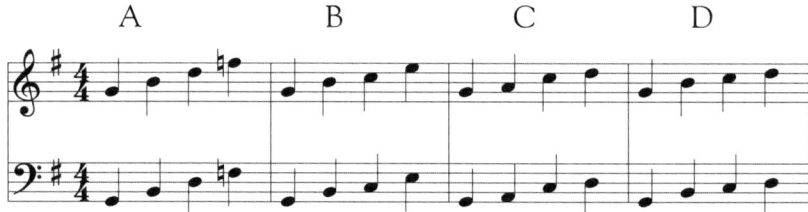

8. Which example is being played?

9. Which example is being played?

10. Which example is being played?

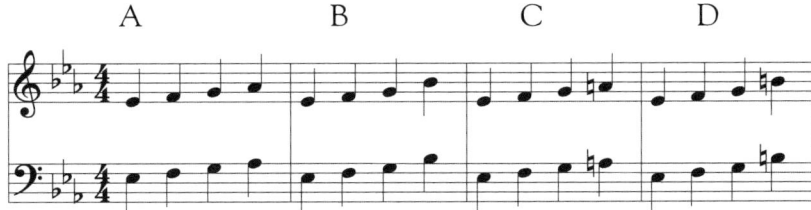

11. Which triad is being played?

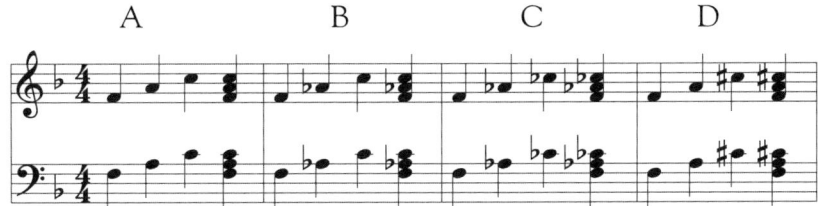

12. Which triad is being played?

13. Which triad is being played?

14. Which triad is being played?

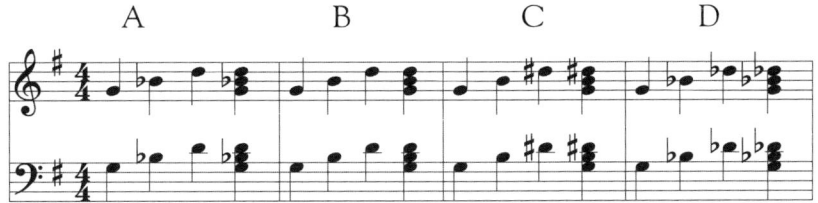

15. Which triad is being played?

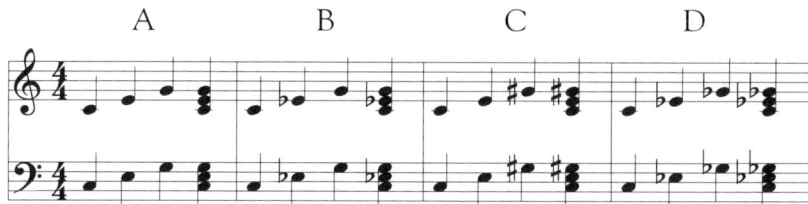

16. Which scale is being played?

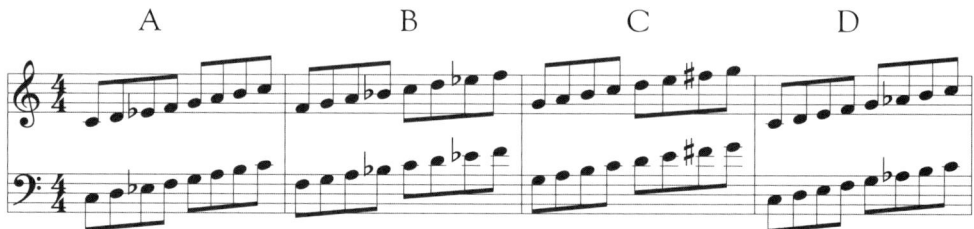

17. Which scale is being played?

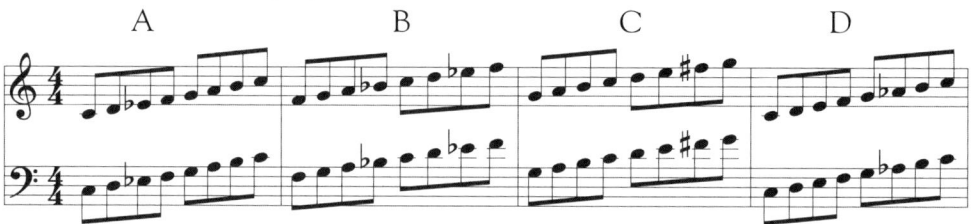

18. Which example is being played?

19. Which example is being played?

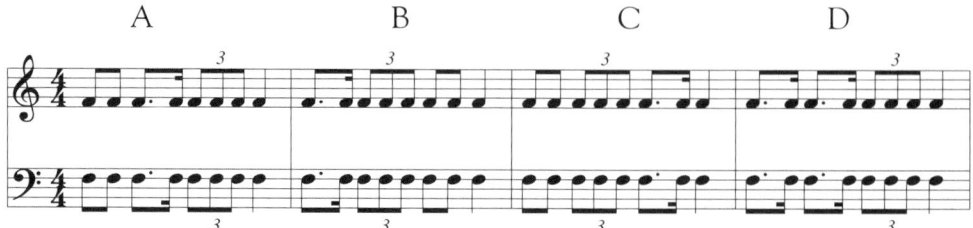

20. Which example is being played?

21. Which example is being played?

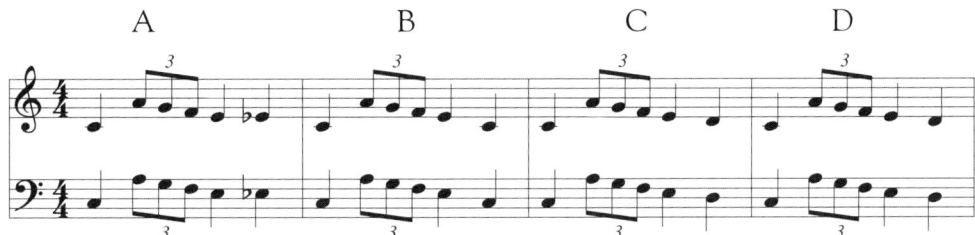

22. Which example is being played?

23. Which example is being played?

24. Which example is correct in both rhythm and pitch?

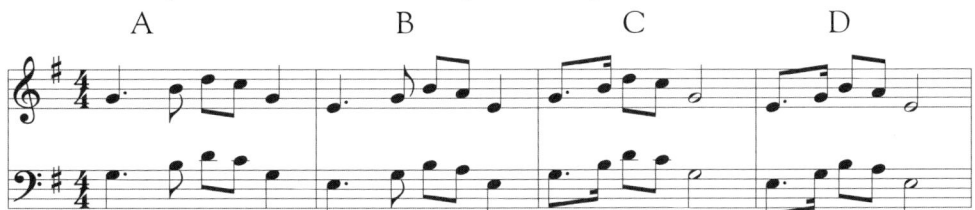

25. Which example is correct in both rhythm and pitch?

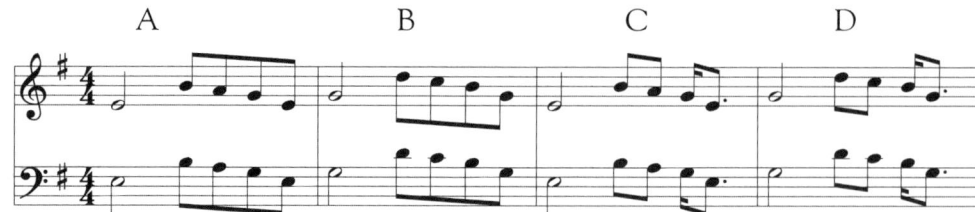

26. Which example is correct in both rhythm and pitch?

27. Which measure in the melody has a mistake in rhythm or pitch?

28. Which measure in the melody has a mistake in rhythm or pitch?

29. Is the melody major or minor?
    Major   Minor

30. Is the melody major or minor?

Major   Minor

31. Is the melody major or minor?

Major   Minor

32. Which interval is being played?

A. Major third   C. Perfect fourth
B. Minor third   D. Perfect fifth

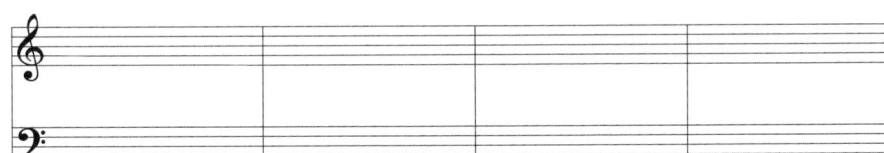

33. Which interval is being played?

A. Perfect fourth   C. Octave (perfect eighth)
B. Perfect fifth   D. Minor sixth

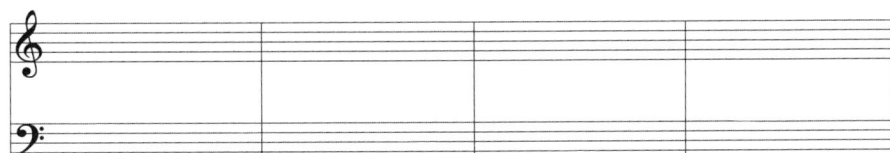

34. Which interval is being played?
   A. Perfect fourth　　　　　C. Major sixth
   B. Major third　　　　　　D. Minor sixth

35. Which interval is being played?
   A. Major third　　　　　　C. Perfect fourth
   B. Minor sixth　　　　　　D. Minor seventh

36. Which interval is being played?
   A. Tritone　　　　　　　　C. Major seventh
   B. Minor seventh　　　　　D. Minor sixth

37. Which interval is being played?
   A. Minor second　　　　　C. Major third
   B. Minor third　　　　　　D. Major second

38. Which triad is being played?
    A. Major
    B. Minor
    C. Diminished
    D. Augmented

39. Which triad is being played?
    A. Major
    B. Minor
    C. Diminished
    D. Augmented

40. Which triad is being played?
    A. Major
    B. Minor
    C. Diminished
    D. Augmented

41. Which triad is being played?
    A. Major
    B. Minor
    C. Diminished
    D. Augmented

42. Which triad is being played?
   A. Major   C. Diminished
   B. Minor   D. Augmented

Appendix F

Websites and Email Addresses

Company/Organization	Physical Address	Telephone	Web/Email Address
Alfred Publishing Co., Inc.	16320 Roscoe Blvd, Suite 100 P.O. Box 1003 Van Nuys, CA 91410	1–818–891–5999	www.alfred.com
GIA Publications, Inc.	7404 South Mason Avenue Chicago, IL 60638	1–800–442–1356 1–708–496–3800	www.giamusic.com
Hinsdale Township High School District Number 86	55th and Grant Streets Hinsdale, Illinois 60521	1–630–655–6100	d86@hinsdale86.org
Illinois Music Educators Association	19747 Wolf Road Suite 201 Mokena, IL 60448–1362	1–708–479–4000	stateoffice@ilmea.org
Illinois State Board of Education	100 N. 1st Street Springfield, IL 62777	1–866–262–6663	www.isbe.state.il.us/ils/ fine_arts/standards.htm
	100 W. Randolph Suite 14–300 Chicago, IL 60601	1–312–814–2220	
JMP USA	SAS Worldwide Headquarters SAS Campus Drive Cary, NC 27513	1–919–677–8000	www.jmp.com
MakeMusic, Inc. (Finale)	7615 Golden Triangle Drive Suite M Eden Prairie, MN 55344–3848	1–952–937–9611	www.finalemusic.com
MENC Music Educators National Conference National Association for Music Education	1806 Robert Fulton Drive Reston, VA 20191	1–800–336–3768	www.menc.org
National Federation of State High Schools Associations	P.O. Box 690 Indianapolis, IN 46206	1–317–972–6900	www.nfhs.org
Pearson Education, Inc.	5601 Green Valley Drive Bloomington, MN 55437	1–800–447–3269	pearsonassessments@ pearson.com

Company/Organization	Physical Address	Telephone	Web/Email Address
Scantron Corporation	34 Parker Irvine California, 92618–1604	1–800–722–6876	www.scantron.com
Sibelius	1407 Oakland Blvd, Suite 103 Walnut Creek, CA 94596	1–888–4-SIBELIUS	www.sibelius.com
SPSS Inc.	233 S. Wacker Drive 11th floor Chicago, IL 60606–6307	1–312–651–3000	www. spss.com

GLOSSARY

alternative assessment	Any assessment technique that uses strategies for collecting and analyzing information different from traditional paper-and-pencil tests.
assessment	The collection, analysis, interpretation, and application of information about student performance or program effectiveness for making educational decisions.
authentic assessment	Assessment techniques that gather information about students' ability to perform tasks that are found in real-world situations.
benchmark	The comparison of student performance against an established standard that provides information about the degree to which the student is making progress toward attaining the standard.
criteria	A description of the standard of performance for a particular task.
criterion-referenced	Determining the level of a student's performance on a body of knowledge or skills that were specified prior to the student's performance of a task.
evaluation	The collection and use of information to make informed educational decisions.
formative assessment	Ongoing assessment within an educational program with the purpose of improving the program as it progresses.
maximum	The highest score in a set of scores.
mean	The arithmetic average of a group of scores.
median	The midpoint of a range of scores (e.g., the 50th percentile).

minimum	The lowest score in a set of scores.
norm	The midpoint in a set of scores taken from a large random sample of individuals where fifty percent of the scores are above the norm and fifty percent are below.
norm-referenced	T value of a student's performance determined by referring to a norm established by a large number of representative individuals that indicates how a student performed in relation to other individuals' previous performances.
performance assessment	An assessment technique that determines a student's ability to perform on assigned tasks rather than on the ability to answer questions.
performance task	A student demonstration that shows ability to handle complex material in real-world situations.
portfolio assessment	A collection of student work used to demonstrate student attainment in a content area. Student progress is determined by reviewing the collected works in light of previously established criteria.
program assessment	The determination of an educational program's strengths and weaknesses through a well-conceived and implemented plan of data collection and analysis.
range	Subtract the minimum from the maximum to obtain the range.
reliability	The consistency of an assessment instrument to obtain comparable scores across time.
rubric	A set of scoring criteria used to determine the value of a student's performance on assigned tasks. The criteria are written so students are able to learn what must be done to improve their performance in the future.

self-assessment	Analyzing and making decisions about one's own performance or abilities.
standard	The content, level, or type of performance expected by students at a particular point in time or stage of development.
standard deviation	Provides a reference of a group of scores to the normal curve; alternatively, it describes the variability or spread of a group of scores.
statistic of relationship/ Pearson Product Moment Correlation	A number ranging from -1.00 to +1.00 that indicates how well two groups of numbers relate to each other, with +1.00 equaling a perfect positive relationship, -1.00 equaling a perfect negative relationship, and 0.00 indicating no relationship.

STATISTICS ABOUT A TEST

reliability	Indicates the measuring consistency of a test, i.e., how consistent scores are in two different administrations of the same test.
split-half reliability	Obtained by computing the Pearson Product Moment Correlation between scores on odd items and scores on even items for each person and then correcting scores using the Spearman-Brown Prophecy Formula.

STATISTICS ABOUT TEST ITEMS

item difficulty	Indicates how difficult an item is. Ranges between 0.0 (no one answered the item correctly) to 1.0 (everyone answered the item correctly).
item discrimination	Indicates how well the item distinguished between those who did well on the test and those who did not.
student assessment	The determination of one or more students' capabilities in a subject matter made from information gathered on meaningful performance tasks that are referenced to well-defined, educationally sound performance criteria.

summative assessment	An assessment performed to determine the overall effectiveness of an educational program.

TEST STATISTICS FOR INDIVIDUALS

z-score	Indicates where a person places on the normal curve.
T score	Indicates a person's score such that an average score is fifty, with every ten points above or below indicating one standard deviation above or below the average of the group.
stanine	Standard nine; indicates a person's score such that an average score is five with every two points above or below indicating one standard deviation above or below the average of the group.

validity	The ability of an assessment instrument to measure what it is supposed to measure. Also, the appropriate use of assessment information and results.

REFERENCES

Arter, Judith A., and Kathleen U. Busick. *Practice with Student-Involved Classroom Assessment*. Portland: Assessment Training Institute, 2001.

Assessment Training Institute. (n.d.) *"Ideas for grant proposal writing."* Resources section of the website of the Assessment Training Institute, Inc., Portland, OR.

Black, Paul, and Dylan Wiliam. *Inside the Black Box: Raising Standards through Classroom Assessment*. Bloomington: Phi Delta Kappa International, 1998.

Chappuis, Stephen, Richard Stiggins, Judith Arter, and Jan Chappuis. *Assessment for Learning: An Action Guide for School Leaders*. Portland: Assessment Training Institute, Inc., 2004.

Covington, Martin V. *Making the Grade: A Self-Worth Perspective on Motivation and School Reform*. New York: Cambridge University Press, 1992.

Crooks, T J. 1988. The impact of classroom evaluation practices on students. Review of Educational Research, 58(4):438–481.

Harnisch, Delwyn L., "Principles and Technologies for Improving Student Learning." Invited keynote lecture, InSITE International Symposium on IT and Education, Kochi University of Technology, Kochi, Japan, 2002.

———, R. Shope, M. Hoback, M. Fryda, and D. Kelberlau. "Connecting high-quality local assessment to teacher leadership." In Ken Jones, ed., *Democratic School Accountability: A Model for School Improvement*. Blue Ridge Summit, PA: Scarecrow Press, 2006.

Hattie, John, and Helen Timperley. "The power of feedback." *Review of Educational Research*, 77(1):81–112, 2007.

"National Standards for Music Education." The National Association for Music Education. http://www.menc.org/publication/books/standards.htm

Seligman, Martin E. *Learned Optimism: How to Change Your Mind and Your Life*. New York: Pocket Books, 1998.

Shepard, Lorrie A. 1991. Interview on assessment issues with Lorrie Shepard. *Educational Researcher*, 20(3), 21–23.

Stiggins, Richard J. *Student-Involved Assessment for Learning*, 4th ed. Upper Saddle River, NJ: Merrill/Prentice Hall, 2005.

Stiggins, Richard J. *Student-Involved Classroom Assessment*. 3rd ed. Columbus, OH: Merrill; Portland: Assessment Training Institute, Inc., 2000.

Stiggins, Richard J., Judith A. Arter, Jan Chappuis, and Stephen Chappuis. *Classroom Assessment for Student Learning: Doing It Right—Using It Well*. Portland, OR: Assessment Training Institute, Inc., 2004.

INDEX

ABOUT THE AUTHORS

Delwyn L. Harnisch received his doctorate in Educational Psychology from the University of Illinois at Urbana-Champaign in 1980. He is a Professor of Educational Psychology at the Department of Teaching, Learning, and Teacher Education, College of Education and Human Sciences, University of Nebraska Lincoln (UNL). With a wealth of background and expertise in measurement, assessment, and program evaluation, Harnisch is the Director of the Assessment and Leadership for Learning Center that provides assessment literacy professional development programs for school teachers and leaders. His thirty years of teaching and research experience has focused on integration of technology into the teaching and learning process. He has authored over 150 research articles, five books, and secured over ten million dollars in grants and contracts. Many of his students are serving as faculty in leading research programs across the U. S. as well as in Japan and China. He has received numerous national and international honors for his research programs and writings, including the most recent Excellence in Classroom Assessment Training Award in Teacher Education for Assessment Cohort Program at University of Nebraska-Lincoln from the National Council of Measurement in Education (NCME).

Paul Kimpton is the Director of Bands and Department Chairman at Hinsdale South High School in Darien, Illinois, and has taught for thirty-two years. He received the Bachelor and Master of Music Education degrees from the University of Illinois, an Administrator's Certificate from Western Illinois University, and a Guidance/Counseling Certificate from Northern Illinois University. Kimpton's teaching experience ranges from rural Minnesota in a town of 900 with ninety in the high school to the Chicago suburbs where high school enrollment is near 2000 students. His thirty years of teaching have given him experience in elementary, junior high, and high school concert band, marching band, jazz band, combo, choir, pit orchestra, music history, AP music theory, class piano, vocal music, and composition. Under his direction, the musical groups at Hinsdale South High School have won over 200 awards for excellence in jazz, concert, percussion, and marching band events through out the U. S. He has written articles for *The Instrumentalist* and *Illinois Music Educators*. Kimpton is in demand as a clinician on music assessment throughout the midwest.